10113695

City of Macon (Ga.)

A Compilation of the Acts of the Legislature Incorporating

the City of Macon, Georgia

and a revision and consolidation of the ordinances passed by the city

council of Macon, to the 3d October, 1862 - Vol. 1

City of Macon (Ga.)

A Compilation of the Acts of the Legislature Incorporating the City of Macon, Georgia
and a revision and consolidation of the ordinances passed by the city council of Macon, to the 3d October, 1862 - Vol. 1

ISBN/EAN: 9783337301941

Printed in Europe, USA, Canada, Australia, Japan

Cover: Foto ©Suzi / pixelio.de

More available books at **www.hansebooks.com**

A COMPILATION

OF THE

ACTS OF THE LEGISLATURE

INCORPORATING THE

CITY OF MACON, GEORGIA:

AND

A REVISION AND CONSOLIDATION

OF THE

ORDINANCES

PASSED BY THE CITY COUNCIL OF MACON,

TO

OCTOBER, 1862.

COMPILED BY RICHARD CURD, CLERK OF COUNCIL.

MACON:

ROSE & CO., PRINTERS.

1862.

CITY GOVERNMENT.

M. S. THOMSON, Mayor.

MEMBERS OF COUNCIL.

JOHN T. BOIFEUILLET, JOHN L. JONES,
JAS. V. GRIER, W. P. GOODALL,
O. F. ADAMS, R. B. BARFIELD,
E. C. GRANNISS, THOS. A. HARRIS.

CITY OFFICERS.

RICHARD CURD, *Clerk and Treasurer.*
GEO. D. LAWRENCE, *Chief Marshal.*
WM. P. ANDERSON, *Keeper of Guard House.*
JOHN J. HARRIS, *Keeper Magazine.*
ROB'T BIRDSONG, *Bridge Keeper.*
STEPHEN MENARD, *Clerk of Market.*
J. A. SIMPSON, *Overseer Street Hands.*
GEO. S. OBEAR, *Chief Engineer Fire Department.*
GEO. W. PRICE, *Assistant " " "*
JOHN BROMLEY, *Keeper City Clock.*
A. BRYDIE, *City Sexton.*
JOHN BERKNER, *Keeper City Hall.*

POLICE.

WM. WRYE, W. S. BAGLEY,
W. J. DAVIS, C. SUMRELL,
J. ANDERSON, HENRY GANTT,
GEO. RAN. JAMES JONES.

CITY CHARTER.

AN ACT TO ALTER AND AMEND THE SEVERAL ACTS INCORPORATING THE CITY OF MACON.

SECTION 1. *Be it enacted by the Senate and House of Representatives of the State of Georgia, in General Assembly met, and it is hereby enacted by the authority of the same,* That the Municipal Government of the city of Macon shall consist of a Mayor and eight Aldermen, who are hereby constituted a body corporate, under the name and style of "The Mayor and Council of the city of Macon," and by that name and style shall have perpetual succession, shall have a common seal, and be capable in law and equity to purchase, have, hold, receive, enjoy, possess, and retain to them and their successors, for the use of the city of Macon, any estate or estates, real or personal, of whatsoever kind or nature within the jurisdictional limits of the city of Macon; and shall, by the said name, be capable to sue, and be sued, in any court of law or equity in this State; and shall succeed to all the rights and liabilities of the present corporation of the city of Macon;* and the corporate limits of the city shall be the same as those now established by law.†

SEC. 2. *Be it further enacted by the authority aforesaid,* That an election shall be held, at the Court House‡ in the city of Macon, on the first Saturday in January§ of each year, for a Mayor and eight Aldermen, to serve for one year, and until their successors are elected and qualified; and the polls of which election shall be opened at nine o'clock in the forenoon, and closed at four o'clock in the afternoon.

SEC. 3. *Be it further enacted, by the authority aforesaid,* That all male white citizens qualified to vote for members of the State

---

* See specifications of general powers under old charter. See page 23.
† Extended—See page 19.
‡ "Or such other place," &c.—See page 15.
§ Now Second Saturday in December—see page 14.

Legislature, and who shall have paid all taxes legally imposed and demanded by the authorities of the city, and shall have resided six months within the jurisdictional limits of said city, and no other person, shall be qualified to vote at said election for Mayor and Aldermen. And in case any person otherwise qualified to vote at said election, shall move into the city after the time for giving in his taxes, and whose name shall not appear on the tax book of the preceding year, he shall, in order to entitle him to vote, report his name to the Clerk of Council, before the opening of the polls, in order that he may be enrolled among the tax paying citizens.

Sec. 4. *And is it further enacted, by the authority aforesaid*, That the said election shall be held under the superintendence of a justice of the peace and two freeholders, or of three freeholders, who shall be appointed by the City Council, at least five days before the election. And each of the said freeholders, before entering upon his duties, shall take an oath before some justice of the peace, that "he will faithfully and impartially conduct said election, and prevent all illegal voting, to the best of his skill and power." And in case the said managers of said election shall have any reasonable doubts as to the qualifications of any voter, they shall have power to administer the following oath: "You do solemnly swear that you have attained the age of twenty-one years; that you are a citizen of the United States, and have resided for the last six months past within the jurisdiction of the Corporation of the city of Macon, and have paid all taxes legally imposed and demanded of you by the City Council of Macon. So help you God." And any person who shall take either of said oaths, and shall have sworn falsely, shall be liable to indictment and punishment for perjury.

Sec. 5. *And be it further enacted, by the authority aforesaid*, That the person or persons who shall receive the highest number of votes at said election for Mayor and Aldermen respectively, shall be declared duly elected.

Sec. 6. *And be it further enacted, by the authority aforesaid*, That in case of any vacancy among the members of Council, either by death, resignation, failure to elect, removal from office, or removal from the city, the Mayor shall advertise a new election, to fill the vacancy. And in case of the death of the Mayor, his resigna-

tion, removal from office, or removal from the city, the City Council shall order an election for filling the vacancy, in each case
giving ten days' notice, in the public gazettes of the city.

SEC. 7. *Be it further enacted, by the authority aforesaid,* That after
the votes for Mayor and Aldermen, at any election, shall have
been counted by the managers, they shall cause two certified
copies of the tally sheets to be made out, one of which shall be
handed over to the Mayor for the time being, and the other shall
be retained by the managers. And so soon as the Mayor as
aforesaid, shall be informed of the result of said election, he shall
cause the persons elected to be notified of the same. And the
persons elected as aforesaid shall attend, on the first Wednesday
thereafter, at the Council Chamber, for the purpose of organizing
the Council. And the Mayor, and each member of the Council,
shall take and subscribe, before a justice of the peace, or justice
of the Inferior Court for the county of Bibb, [the following oath:]
" I, A. B., do solemnly swear, that I will well and truly perform
the duties of [Mayor or member of the Council, as the case may
be] of the City Council of Macon, by adopting such measures as
shall, in my judgment, be best calculated to promote the general
welfare of the inhabitants of the city of Macon, and the common
thereof; so help me God;" and shall forthwith enter upon the
duties of their offices.

SEC. 8. *Be it further enacted, by the authority aforesaid,* That in
case the Mayor, or any member of the Council, while in office,
shall be guilty of any willful neglect, mal-practice, or abuse of
the power confided to him, he shall be subject to be indicted before the Superior Court of the county of Bibb; and on conviction,
shall be fined in a sum not exceeding one hundred dollars; and
shall moreover be removed from office. And the said fine shall
paid to the City Treasurer, for the use of the city.

SEC. 9. *Be it further enacted, by the authority aforesaid,* That no
person shall be eligible as Mayor of the city of Macon, unless he
be a free white man, of the age of twenty-five years, a citizen of
the United States, and shall have resided in said city for two
years immediately preceding his election. And no person shall
be eligible as a member of the City Council, unless he shall have
attained the age of twenty-one years, and shall have the other
qualifications specified in the case of Mayor.

Sec. 10. *Be it further enacted, by the authority aforesaid.* That the said Mayor and Council of the city of Macon shall have power to appoint a Marshal, and such officers of the city as they may deem necessary and proper, and shall have power to regulate the time, mode, and manner of electing said officers,* to establish their fees and salaries; to take their bonds; to prescribe their duties and their oaths; and to remove them from office for a breach, neglect or incapacity to discharge the said duties, at their discretion.

Sec. 11. *And be it further enacted, by the authority aforesaid,* That the Mayor and members of the Council shall be bound to keep the peace, and shall be, ex officio, justices of the peace, so far as to enable them to issue warrants for offences committed within the jurisdiction of the city of Macon; and shall have power on examination, to commit the offender or offenders to jail, or bail them, if the offence be bailable, to appear before the Superior Court of the county of Bibb.†

Sec. 12. *And be it further enacted, by the authority aforesaid,* That the said Mayor and Council of the city of Macon, or a majority of them, shall have power and authority to levy and collect a poll tax on all free white persons within the city of Macon, between the ages of twenty-one and sixty years; upon all free persons of color; and also upon all slaves owned or hired within the city of Macon. They shall also have power to levy and collect a tax upon all and every species of property, real or personal, within the limits of the city of Macon; upon banking or insurance capital employed in the city; upon bank or insurance agents, and professional men; upon factors, brokers, and venders of lottery tickets; thus to raise such sum or sums of money as may be necessary for the support and good government of the city, in all its internal regulations, and for the payment of the debts thereof. *Provided,* That the tax levied upon real estate, and stock in trade, shall not exceed fifty cents on every one hundred dollars in value.

Sec. 13. *Be it further enacted, by the authority aforesaid,* That the Mayor and Council of the city of Macon shall have power and authority to levy, in addition to the other taxes, a tax of not ex-

---

* See page 16   † See amendment, page 16

ceeding three dollars, upon each and every white person and slave in the city of Macon, between the ages of twenty-one and forty-five years, as a street tax. *Provided*, That the person so taxed may relieve himself of said tax by working on the streets for six days, under the direction and control of the Marshal of the city.

SEC. 14. *Be it further enacted, by the authority aforesaid,* That the said Mayor and Council of the city of Macon shall have full power and authority to remove, or cause to be removed, any buildings, posts, steps, fence, or other obstruction or nuisance in the public streets, lanes, alleys, sidewalks, or public squares in said city. They shall further have power to establish a market or markets, in the city of Macon, and to pass such ordinances as may be proper and necessary for the regulation of the same.— They shall have power to license, regulate and control all taverns and public houses within the city. They shall have power to regulate all butcher pens and slaughter houses within the city, and remove the same if they shall become nuisances, or injurious to the health of the city. They shall have power to license drays, and regulate the same. And further, the said Mayor and Council shall have full power and control over all livery stables, pumps, fire companies, and engines within the said city.

SEC. 15. *Be it further enacted, by the authority aforesaid,* That the said Mayor and Council of the city of Macon shall have power, upon proof of the existence and maintenance of any house of ill fame, or bawdy-house, within the city, to cause occupants thereof to be forcibly removed without the city, if they shall refuse to leave the city after five days' notice.

SEC. 16. *Be it further enacted, by the authority aforesaid,* That the said Mayor and Council of the city of Macon shall have power to license, appoint annually, as many auctioneers or vendue masters for the city, as they may deem proper, and to receive from each one the sum of fifty dollars, as fixed by law; and they shall further have power to levy a tax upon all goods sold on commission, or at auction, in said city, to be paid by the auctioneer.

SEC. 17. *Be it further enacted, by the authority aforesaid,* That the said Mayor and Council of the city of Macon shall have the sole and exclusive right of granting licenses to retail liquors in the

2

city of Macon, and of fixing the rate of such licenses, and the
terms upon which they shall be issued; of declaring said licenses
void, when said terms are not complied with. They shall also
have power to license, regulate and control all ten pin alleys,
within the city, and to remove the same when they become nuisances to the neighborhood.

SEC. 18. *Be it further enacted,* That the said Mayor and Council of the city of Macon shall have power to tax all theatrical
performances, exhibitions, or shows of any kind, within the cor.
porate limits of said city.

SEC. 19. *Be it further enacted,* That the said Mayor and Council shall have power to pass all ordinances, rules and regulations
necessary and proper for the good government and subjection of
all slaves, and free persons of color, within the city. And the
Marshals, and such other persons as the said Mayor and Council shall appoint, are hereby vested with the full power and authority of patrols in said city.

SEC. 20. *Be it further enacted, by the authority aforesaid,* That the
said Mayor and Council of the city of Macon, shall have power
to remove any forge or smith shop, when, in their opinion, it shall
be necessary to ensure safety against fire. They shall have power to cause any stove, stove-pipe, or other thing which shall endanger the city as to fire, to be removed or remedied, as their
prudence shall dictate.

SEC. 21. *Be it further enacted,* That the said Mayor and Council of the city of Macon, shall, during the month of April in
each year, appoint nine fit and proper persons, who shall constitute the Board of Health, five of whom shall constitute a quorum, to meet weekly, or as often as may be necessary; to visit
all and every part of the city, and to report to the Council all
nuisances which are likely to endanger the health of the city, or
of any neighborhood. And the said Mayor and Council shall
have power, upon the report of the Board of Health, to cause
any such nuisance to be abated, and their recommendations car-
ried out in a summary manner, at the expense of the party whose
act or negligence caused such nuisances, or of the owner of the
premises, as the Council shall elect.

SEC. 22. *Be it further enacted, by the authority aforesaid,* That the
said Mayor and Council of the city of Macon, shall have the

power, upon the recommendation of the Board of Health, to cause the owners of lots within the said city, to drain the same, or to fill the same to the levels of the streets or alleys on which said lot or lots are fronting. Also, to compel the owner or owners of cellars occasionally holding water, to cause the same to be emptied of the water, or filled up, if necessary. And in case the owner of said lot or lots shall fail or refuse, after reasonable notice to him or his agent, to comply with the requirements of the said Mayor and Council, by filling up said lots or cellars, or by draining the same, it shall be lawful for the said Mayor and Council to employ some person to do the same; and for the amount so expended, the City Treasurer shall forthwith issue an execution against the owner of said property, to be collected from said lot, or any other property belonging to him; and a sale under said execution, by the Marshal, shall pass the title to the property sold, as completely as a sale under a judgment and execution by the Sheriff.

SEC. 23. *And be it further enacted, by the authority aforesaid*, That the said Mayor and Council of the city of Macon, shall have power to fill any vacancies which may occur in the Board of Health; and this act may be pleaded, and sh ll be a complete defence to any action brought against the sa d Mayor and Council, or either of them, for any act done by them under its provisions, and of the ordinances passed in pursuance of it.

SEC. 24. *And be it further enacted, by the authority aforesaid*, That the said Mayor and Council of the city of Macon, shall have power to take up and impound, any horses, mules, cattle, or hogs running at large within the limits of said city; and to pass such ordinances as may be deemed by them necessary, for the proper regulation of stock within the city.

SEC. 25. *And be it further enacted, by the authority aforesaid*, That the said Mayor and Council of the city of Macon, shall have power to establish and regulate a City Guard, who shall have the right to take up all disorderly persons; all persons committing, or attempting to commit, any crime, and commit them to the Guard House or common Jail of Bibb county, to await their trial the next day. And the said Guard shall also have the power and authority of patrols over slaves, and free persons of color.

SEC. 26. *And be it further enacted by the authority aforesaid,* That the said Mayor and Council of the city of Macon, shall have the power and authority, in case of riot, rebellion, or insurrection in the city of Macon. to call out the several volunteer companies, to aid in suppressing such riot, rebellion. or insurrection. And it shall be the duty of the captains, and other officers of said companies, to obey the orders of said Mayor and Council, for said purpose; and for disobedience, they and each of them, shall forfeit their commissions.

SEC. 27. (This section repealed by act of 1857.) See page 16.

SEC. 28. *And be it further enacted, by the authority aforesaid,* That no person, or body corporate, shall at any time hereafter, open, lay out, or extend any street, alley, lane, or open square, contrary to the original plan of said city, without the consent of three-fourths of the Council, at a regular meeting. And any application of this kind shall be published for one month before the final action of the Council thereon.

SEC. 29. *And be it further enacted, by the authority aforesaid,* That the said Mayor and Council of the city of Macon, shall have the power and authority to pass all rules and ordinances necessary for the protection and preservation of the bridge across the Ocmulgee river at Macon, and shall regulate the tolls of the same, and damage or injury done said brige shall subject the offender to indictment and punishment in the Superior Court of Bibb county, for malicious mischief.

SEC. 30. *And be it further enacted, by the authority aforesaid,* That the said Mayor and Council of the city of Macon, shall have the power to appoint Inspectors of the Weights and Measures in use in said city, and to fix fees for the same, which shall be paid by the parties using said Weights or Measures.

SEC. 31. *And be it further enacted, by the authority aforesaid,* That it shall be the duty of the Marshal of the city, upon notice in writing from the Mayor, or any member of Council, to prosecute all the offenders against the laws of this State for crimes committed within the limits of the city of Macon. And in case any offence shall be committed in the presence of said Marshal, or within his knowledge, it shall be his duty to prosecute without such notice.

SEC. 32. *And be it further enacted,* That the said Mayor and

Council of the city of Macon, shall have power to lease or sell, any portion of the Town Common, not leased or sold, which they shall deem proper, and to appropriate the proceeds to the use of said city.

SEC. 33. *And be it further enacted, by the authority aforesaid*, That the said Mayor and Council of the city of Macon, shall have power to appoint assessors,* to value the real estate of said city, for taxation; and all taxes levied by said Mayor and Council, shall be collected as follows: An execution shall be issued by the Treasurer of the city, directed to the Marshal of the city, against the estate, real and personal, of the defaulter; and the Marshal shall proceed to levy the same; and after advertising for thirty days, shall sell the property levied on, before the Court House door of the county of Bibb, on a regular Sheriff sale day, and between the legal hours of Sheriff's sales. The said Marshal shall put up said property, and shall offer the same in parcels, until he gets a bid sufficient to pay the taxes due, and shall then knock off the property to the purchaser, and make him a deed, which shall be as effectual, to pass the title, as the deed of the person against whom said execution was issued.

SEC. 34. *And be it further enacted, by the authority aforesaid*, That a Clerk and Treasurer of the city of Macon shall be elected by the people of said city qualified to vote for Mayor and Aldermen, at the regular election in January,† and shall serve for one year. He shall give bond in a sum of five thousand dollars, with two good securities, conditioned for the faithful performance of his duties as Clerk and Treasurer of said city, and shall take an oath that he will, to the best of his skill and power, perform the duties of his office, without favor or affection.

SEC. 35. *And be it further enacted by the authority aforesaid*, That the acts heretofore passed, incorporating the city of Macon, together with all laws, and parts of laws, militating against this act, be, and the same are hereby repealed.

Passed, December 27th, 1847.

---

*Repealed as to "assessors." See page 14.
†Now December. See page 14.

AMENDMENTS TO CITY CHARTER.

Be it enacted, &c., That from and after the passage of this act, so much of an act entitled "an act to alter and amend the several acts incorporating the city of Macon," approved December 27th, 1847, as authorizes and empowers the Mayor and Council of the city of Macon to appoint assessors to value the real estate of said city for taxation, be and the same is hereby repealed.

Be it further enacted, &c., That hereafter it shall be the duty of all tax payers and owners of real estate in the city of Macon, and they are hereby required, to make their returns under oath of the value of their property in said city, held in their own right or in the right of others: *Provided, always, however,* That the Mayor and any two members of the Council, selected for that purpose, together with the Clerk of the Council, shall have power to supervise all returns made by tax payers, and if in their opinion any of such returns are incorrect in fixing the value of the property in the same, then to correct any such returns thus incorrectly made, by affixing or assessing such higher value as in their opinion may be proper and right.

Passed, February 21, 1850.

Be it enacted, &c., That from and after the passage of this act, the police regulations of the city of Macon shall extend, and be of force over the entire tract of land, lying immediately below, and adjoining said city, known as the reserve, set apart by the act of the twenty-third day of December, eighteen hundred and twenty-six.

Be it further enacted, &c., That after the election to be held on the first Saturday in January, eighteen hundred and fifty-two, for a Mayor and eight Aldermen of the city of Macon, the next election for said officers, and also for Clerk and Treasurer of said city, shall be held on the second Saturday in December, eighteen hundred and fifty-two, and annually thereafter, on the second Saturday in December, of each year.

And be it further enacted, &c., That the Marshal and Deputies of the city of Macon shall, after their election and qualification, be under the exclusive control of the Mayor and Council, and may be dismissed from office at any time, for mal-practice in office, or neglect of duty, by the vote of a majority of the members present, at any regular meeting 6f Council, and not to be re eligible, during the time for which they may have been elected.

And be it further enacted, &c., That in the event of a vacancy in the office of Marshal and Deputies, by removal, death or otherwise, the Mayor or Council may order another election upon giving ten days' public notice.

And be it further enacted, &c., That the Mayor and Council of the city of Macon, and their successors in office, shall have power to subscribe for Stock in the Macon Canal Company, and to impose a tax upon the real estate of said city to pay for the same: *Provided*, The consent of a majority of the owners of said real estate shall have been first obtained, in such manner as the Mayor and Council may prescribe.

And be it further enacted, &c., That should the Board of Health of said city, neglect or decline to attend to the duties imposed upon them, the Mayor and Council shall act as said Board of Health, and have the power to remove all nuisances that may be prejudicial to the health of said city, as is now provided by law.

Passed, January 22d, 1852.

Be it enacted, &c., That the second section of an act incorporating the city of Macon be amended as follows: after "Court House," add—"or such other place as the Mayor and Council may direct."

Passed, December 28, 1853.

And be it further enacted, &c., That said Mayor and Council shall have power to establish and fix fire limits, and from time to time, in their discretion, to extend and enlarge the same, within which fire limits, when so established, it shall not be lawful for any one to erect other than fire-proof buildings, or structures of any kind whatever, and should any one erect, or cause to be erected, within such fire limits so established, any buildings or other structures of any kind, other than fire-proof, the said Mayor and Council, after giving five days' notice, shall cause the same to be removed at the expense of the owners of such build-

ings or other structures; to be collected by execution as in other
cases, and said Mayor and Council shall have power to determine what buildings or other structures are or are not fire-proof.

Be it further enacted. That the said Mayor and Council shall
have authority, on the recommendation of a majority of citizens
in public meeting, to subscribe for the stock of railroads, or such
other internal improvements, or of such as may be for the interest and advantage of the city of Macon, to borrow money on the
faith and credit of the city to pay the same, and to impose a special tax to meet such debt so created: *Provided,* That the special
tax being authorized, shall not exceed one-half of one per cent.
in any one year: *And Provided,* The aggregate amount of in-
debtedness of said city hereby authorized, shall not at any one
time exceed two hundred and fifty thousand dollars.

Passed, December 28, 1853.

And be it further enacted, That the Marshals and such other
officers as the City Council of Macon may deem necessary in the
government of said city, shall hereafter be elected by the said
Council at the first meeting of Council in each year.

Passed, February 20, 1854.

Be it enacted, &c., That from and after the passage of this Act
the twenty seventh section of the Act entitled an Act to alter
and amend the several Acts incorporating the city of Macon,
approved December 27, 1847, be and the same is hereby repealed, and in lieu thereof shall read as follows: The Mayor of
the city of Macon shall have power to impose fines for the violation of any ordinance of the city passed in accordance with its
charter to the amount of one hundred dollars, and to imprison
offenders in the common jail of Bibb county for the space of one
month. The said fine, after being regularly assessed, shall be
collected by execution to be issued by the City Treasurer
against the estate of said offender, if any to be found; if none,
the offender may be imprisoned as before provided.

Be it enacted, &c., That in all cases of encroachment upon
street lands or alleys in said city, the said Mayor and Council
shall have power to remove the same upon reasonable notice, or
to permit and sanction the same for a fair and reasonable com-

pensation in money, to be paid into the City Treasury, said Mayor and Council having due regard to the interests of the property holders who may be affected thereby.

He it enacted, &c., That the said Mayor and Council, or a majority of the Council, shall have power to elect a Mayor *pro tem.*, who shall be clothed thereby with all the rights, privileges and duties of the Mayor elect when and during the sickness or absence of the Mayor, upon taking the usual oath and not otherwise. And if the Mayor, *pro tem.*, as well as the Mayor elected by the people, should both be unable from any cause to attend to their duties, the Council shall elect another Mayor, *pro tem.*, who shall thereby be clothed with all the rights, powers and duties of Mayor of the city, upon taking the usual oath, and who shall serve only during the absence of the Mayor. A judgment of acquittal or conviction by said Mayor may be and shall be plead in bar in any court for the same offence provided said Mayor has jurisdiction.

(Repealing clause.)

Passed, December 22, 1857.

SPECIAL ACTS RELATIVE TO THE CITY OF MACON.

TO PRESERVE THE TIMBER ON THE RESERVE.

Be it enacted, &c., That for the purpose of preserving the standing timber immediately below the improved part of the town of Macon, for the preservation of the health of the inhabitants of said town, all the land within the plat below Seventh street, together with a space of six hundred yards below, and a space of three hundred yards on the South-western or outer side thereof, is vested hereby in the corporate authority of said town for the time being. *Provided,* That if the said corporate authority shall sell, lease, or in any way alien or encumber the said land, or any part thereof, or shall offer the same in any manner, or for any purpose to be inhabited, the land, or portions of land so aliened, encumbered or inhabited, shall thenceforward revest in the State. *Provided,* also, That nothing in this act contained, shall prevent

3

the State from resuming the said land, if in the opinion of any
future Legislature, the public good should require such resumption.

And be it further enacted, That if any person shall cut down or
or kill, or shall direct or cause to be cut down or killed, any tree
of more than two inches diameter, at two feet from the ground,
other than pine trees, on any of the land within the town plat of
the said town below Seventh street, and within a space of six
hundred yards below, and three hundred yards on the South-
western, or outer side thereof, such person shall be liable to indictment, and on conviction, shall be held guilty of malicious
mischief, and shall be punished at the discretion of the court, by
confinement in the common Jail of the county, and by fine payable to the corporation of Macon.

And be it further enacted, That (if) any slave, or any person in
the employment of others shall violate this act, it shall be presumptive evidence of the same being done by direction of the
owner or employer. *Provided,* That no person shall be punished
upon such presumptive evidence alone, otherwise than by fine;
but if it shall satisfactorily appear that such offence was not
committed by the direction or assent of such owner or employer,
then the person actually committing the offence, shall be liable,
if a white person, to trial and punishment as provided by this
act; and if a person of color, to such punishment as the ordinances of the said town may have imposed. But nothing in
this act shall prohibit the exercise by the Inferior Court of their
ordinary and legal jurisdiction in laying out and opening, or al-
tering necessary roads, or shall restrict the said corporation, or
any legal authority, from digging any necessary drains, or ca-
nals, or shall be held to restrain or abridge, in other respects
than herein mentioned, the authority of the agent, for the time
being, of the public service.

Passed, December 23, 1826.

Be it enacted, &c., That for the preservation of the health of
the inhabitants of the city of Macon, and to prevent the spread
of malaria by cutting and felling of timber on said reserve,
thereby endangering the health of said city, that all that plat of
land which by an act " approved December 23, 1826," is vested

for the time being in the corporate authorities of said city, be and the same is hereby vested in said corporate authorities.— *Provided*, That if said authorities should at any time sell, lease, or in any way alien said land, or should offer to sell, alien or convey said land, the same shall thenceforth re-vest in and become the property of the State.

Be it further enacted, THat the said corporate authorities shall not cut down, or cause to be cut down, or killed, any tree or trees in said reserve, only so far as shall be necessary to make roads and ways through the same for their benefit and improvement.

(Conflicting laws repealed.)

Passed, March 6, 1856.

Be it enacted, &c., That from and immeeiately after the passage of this act, the Mayor and Council of Macon shall have liberty, power and authority to lease to John S. Richardson, his heirs and assigns for ten years, with the privilege of renewing on the same terms, a portion of the Common of the city of Macon, known as Napier's Old Field, containing about eighty-seven (87) acres, more or less, he paying therefor the sum of two hundred dollars per annum for rent: *Provided*, Nothing shall be so construed as to authorize said John S. Richardson to destroy or injure the original forest growth thereon, if any.

Passed, December 20, 1853.

TO EXTEND THE LIMITS OF THE TOWN OF MACON.

Be it enacted, &c., That from and after the promulgation of this act, the one-acre lots, on the East side of the Ocmulgee river, opposite the town of Macon, in the county of Bibb, be, and the same are hereby, declared to be within the corporate limits of said town, and that the said one-acre lots shall, and are hereby declared to be subject to all the ordinances and police regulations of the corporation of the town of Macon.

Passed, December 19, 1829.

Be it enacted, &c., That the jurisdictional limits of the town of Macon, shall extend on the East side of the Ocmulgee river, from a line drawn parallel with First-street, northwardly, as far as the present authorized jurisdictional limits, thence on a line eastwardly until it intersects a line running parallel with Seventh-street, until it reaches a point northwardly as far as the present authorized limits of said town of Macon.

Passed, December 26, 1832.

Be it enacted, &c., That from and after the passage of this act the corporate limits of the city of Macon be, and the same are hereby, extended so as to include within the same, lots numbers three and four in block L, being part of fractional lot number fifty-nine, on the East side of the Macon reserve.*

Passed, December 29, 1838.

TRADING WITH SLAVES.†

Be it enacted, &c., That no person living within the corporate limits of said town of Macon, shall sell spirituous liquors in any quantity whatever, within said limits, to a slave, without a ticket from his or her owner, overseer or employer, specially authorizing him or her to purchase the same, under the penalty of thirty dollars.

And be it further enacted, That all offenders against the foregoing section shall be prosecuted in the Superior Court, and upon conviction, the fine shall go one-half to the county, and the other half to the informer, except when the prosecution shall be commenced and conducted by the Marshal, under the direction of the Corporation, and in that case the whole of the fine shall be paid into the Treasury of said Corporation, and become part of its funds.

And be it further enacted, That said Corporation shall be vigilant in having all persons committing offences within the corporate limits of said town against the laws of this State prohibiting the trading with slaves, prosecuted for the same; and on conviction of any offender, prosecuted at the instance of said Corporation, the fine imposed by the Court shall go to and become part of the funds of said Corporation.

Passed, December 23, 1830.

---

* Also, over the "reserve." See page 18.
† This Act probably superceded, if not repealed, by Sec. 19 of Charter of 1847.

Be it enacted, &c., That the proprietors of said bridge for the time being shall have power to demand and receive the following rates of toll, viz:

For every Four Wheel Pleasure Carriage.................... ....50 cts.
For every Road Wagon......................................37½
For every Light Wagon or Gig.............................25
For every Jersey Wagon or Cart...........................12½
For every Man and Horse.......................... .... 6¼
For every led Horse, Mule, &c................................ 3

And for all other Stock, two cents a head.

Passed, December 20, 1828.

Be it enacted, &c., That it shall be the duty of the Commissioners, or a majority of them heretofore appointed to survey and sell the public reserves and bridge across the Ocmulgee river, at Macon; to proceed to sell and transfer to the Corporation of the town of Macon, and their successors in office, said bridge, immediately after the expiration of the present lease, together with the use of one acre of land, on the Eastern bank of said river, to be used as one of the butments, (being the same lately surveyed for that purpose,) and the like use of as much of Fifth-street as may be necessary for the butment of the bridge, for the sum of twenty-five thousand dollars. *Provided*, Said Corporation shall pay to said Commissioners one-tenth part of the above named sum, in cash, or in current bills of chartered banks of this State, and execute a bond, payable to the Governor, for the use of the State, conditioned for the payment of the residue of the purchase, in like money, in nine equal annual installments.

And be it further enacted, That the Commissioners issue to the Corporation a certificate, stating the terms of purchase, which certificate shall not be transferable; on the payment of which purchase money, a grant of the bridge, its privileges and appurtenances, shall issue to the aforesaid corporation, on the payment of four dollars and fifty cents, for office fees; but no grant thereof shall be issued until all the installments shall have been paid.

And for the better securing the payment of said money,

Be it further enacted, That if said Corporation, or their successors in office, shall fail to pay any one of the installments within sixty days of the time prescribed by this Act, the said bridge shall revert to the State, and the Corporation shall be divested of all right, claim, or title to said bridge; and the amount paid to the State for the same.

And be it further enacted, That the said Corporation shall have the perpetual and exclusive privilege of keeping up a bridge at that place; and no bridge or ferry across said river shall be erected, established, or allowed, within three miles therefrom, within a direct line, which may or could in any wise interfere with the said bridge, by diminishing the profit or value thereof.

And be it further enacted, That the said Corporation, when it shall have become the purchaser of said bridge, shall not be permitted to collect toll for any wagon or other carriage loaded with cotton, or corn, under the penalty heretofore mentioned; but in all other cases, the Corporation and its successors in office may demand and collect such tolls as are allowed in the Act relating to this subject.

Passed, December 20, 1828.

Whereas, Pursuant to said recited Act, the said City Council of Macon became the purchasers of the bridge at Macon, for the sum of twenty-five thousand dollars, which sum was secured by the payment of one tenth part thereof, in cash, by a bond payable to the Governor, for the use of the State, conditioned for the payment of the residue of the purchase money in nine equal annual installments.

And whereas, The one half of the entire purchase money has been paid by the said City Council, according to contract, since which time the said bridge has been swept away and destroyed, by an irresistable flood, despite of the utmost exertions; for as much as said bridge is of great public utility, the rebuilding of which has been projected by said City Council, on a more perfect and permanent plan, at a great expense,

Therefore, be it enacted, &c., That from and after the passage of this Act, it shall and may be lawful for the Central Bank, or its officers, and they are hereby required, to cancel and deliver up to the City Council of Macon, their agent, or attorney, the bond or bonds executed and given by them for the payment of the said purchase money, pursuant to said recited Act.

Provided nevertheless, That before said cancelling shall take place, the said City Council, their agent, or attorney, shall tender, pay, and deliver to said Central Bank, or its officers, a bond or bonds, payable to the Governor, for the use of the State, and his successors in office, for a sum equal to double the amount of said purchase money, now unpaid, conditioned for the payment of what may now remain unpaid of the original purchase money, in five equal installments, the first of which shall arise and fall due ten years after the day on which the installment of the original bond or bonds, so directed to be cancelled, shall arise and fall due, by the terms of said bond, from and after the date thereof; the remaining installments successively thereafter, without computing interest thereon.

Be it enacted, &c., That so much of the said recited Acts as requires said bridge at Macon to revert and become the property of the State, on failure of said City Corporation, or their successors in office, to pay any of the installments therein specified, in terms of said Act, be, and the same is hereby repealed; and the forfeiture and reversion therein and thereby specified, shall obtain, arise, and attach on the failure of said Corporation to pay any of the annual installments specified or set forth, or to be set forth, in the renewal bond herein provided for.

Passed, December 23, 1833.

TO PREVENT BRICK-YARDS, &C., ON THE RESERVE.

Be it enacted, &c., That any person keeping up a brick-yard or other nuisance on the town reserve, as described in the first section of an Act to preserve the timber in the vicinity of the town of Macon, for the preservation of the inhabitants thereof, passed the 23d of December, 1826, shall be prosecuted for the same before the Superior Court of Bibb county by the Marshal of the city of Macon; and on conviction, shall be fined in a sum of not less than one hundred, nor more than five hundred dollars; and each day the nuisance is kept up, shall constitute a new and distinct offence.

Passed, December 20, 1834.

GENERAL POWERS OF COUNCIL, UNDER OLD CHARTER.

That said City Council of Macon, shall also be vested with full power and authority, in addition to the power and authority already granted, from time to time, under their common seal, to make and establish such by-laws, rules, and ordinances, respecting streets, lanes, alleys, and open courts, the market, wharves, and public houses, carriages, wagons, carts, drays, livery stables, pumps, buckets, fire engines, and for the regulating of disorderly people, negroes and free persons of color, and in general, every by-law or regulation that shall appear requisite and necessary for the security, welfare, health, and convenience of said city, or for preserving the peace, order and good government of the same; and they are also vested with all powers and authorities, within the jurisdiction of said city, which by law are vested in the Commissioners of roads and streets.

ORDINANCES.

ELECTION AND QUALIFICATION OF OFFICERS.

SECTION 1. The Mayor and Council shall, at their first meeting in December, in each year, or as soon thereafter as practicable, elect by ballot the following officers: a Chief Marshal and one or more Deputy Marshals, Overseer of street hands, Keeper of Magazine, Keeper of Guard House, Bridge Keeper, Clerk of Market, and City Surveyor; which officers shall serve for one year, and until their successors are elected and qualified. They shall be qualified by the Mayor, or some Justice of the Peace, and shall be subject to be removed by the Council, for malpractice, inattention, incompetency, or inefficiency in the discharge of the duties of their offices.

SEC. 2. The bonds of the several officers required by the ordinances of the city, shall be submitted to and approved by the Council, who shall determine upon the responsibility of sureties tendered. And the Council, or a majority of them, may at their discretion, from time to time, whenever the interest of the city shall require it, exact additional security, or a new bond. And in case any officer elected shall fail or refuse to give bond, as before required, or shall fail to give additional security, or a new bond, when required, his office shall be declared vacant, and the Council shall proceed to fill the vacancy, at such time as they may deem proper.

THE MAYOR.

The Mayor shall have a general superintendence of the affairs of the city. He shall preside at all meetings of Council, vote in all elections for officers, and give the casting vote in cases of a tie. It shall be his duty to see that all laws, ordinances, and rules of Council are observed and enforced. He shall hear summarily complaints lodged against persons by any officer of the city, and dispose of the same, if for minor offences, by the imposition of fines, or in his discretion, cause offenders to be bound over to the Superior Court of Bibb county for trial. He shall give to the City Council four weeks' notice of his intended resignation, or absence from the State, and shall not leave the State, without the consent of two-thirds of the Aldermen. *Provided,*

4

nevertheless, in case of emergency, the four weeks' notice may be dispensed with by Council, so far as to permit his resignation, or absence from the State.

CLERK AND TREASURER.

SECTION. 1. The Clerk and Treasurer shall be sworn in by the Mayor, at the first meeting of Council after his election. He shall give a bond, with two or more satisfactory securities, in the sum of five thousand dollars, for the faithful discharge of his duties, the sufficiency of his security to be determined upon by Council; and at their option his bond shall be increased or strengthened. It shall be his duty to attend all meetings of the City Council, to keep the minutes, and record the same. He shall receive the returns of all persons liable to taxation, according to the terms and conditions of the annual Tax Act of the city, administering to each and every person the oath prescribed in said Act, and make a full alphabetical digest of all such returns; and in all cases of defaulters, it shall be his duty to assess a double tax, when they shall fail to make their tax returns within the time prescribed by Council. It shall be his duty to issue all summonses and processes, and all subpoenas to command the attendance of witnesses, that may be necessary in the enforcement of the rules, regulations, and ordinances of the City Council. He shall issue all licenses, and keep a record thereof, and all badges and permits authorised by the Council.

SEC. 2. It shall be his duty to receive, keep and pay out all moneys belonging to the city, keeping regular books, showing his receipts and payments. He shall pay no money without a warrant, duly passed by Council, and signed by the Mayor, authorising the same; and each and every warrant shall be filed by him, as a voucher. His books, accounts, vouchers, &c., shall at all times be open to the Mayor and Council, for examination and inspection; and he shall make out and submit to Council a quarterly report of all his receipts and disbursements. He shall place in the hands of the principal Marshal, or Deputy Marshals, all executions for taxes, taking a receipt, and making settlements with them therefor, and report to the Council any neglect of the Marshals in collecting the same. He shall act as Clerk of the Board of Health, attend their meetings, keep a record of their proceedings, and report the same to the first regular meeting of Council, receiving for his compensation one-fourth of the fines that may be imposed and collected at the instance of the Board of Health. All deeds, leases, and other instruments executed by the Council shall be attested by him, and he shall affix thereto the public seal of the city, of which he shall be the Custodian. For any neglect of duty, he shall be liable to such penalty as the Mayor and City Council may deem proper to inflict, *provided* a sufficient excuse is not given.

Sec. 3. In addition to his salary, he shall be entitled to the following fees, viz.:

For entering conviction of any person and recording fine,...... .... $ 50
" drawing warrant for any person, by order of Council or any member thereof............. 50
" issuing execution, in any case,........................ 30
" drawing recognizance,................................... 62¼
" drawing Commitimus by order of the Mayor,................. 31¼
" drawing bond, and issuing license to retailers,................. 1 00
" drawing bond, and issuing license for drays,.................. 1 00
" numbers of drays, each..................................... 25
" drawing and attesting lease or deeds for city lots,.............. 2 00
" badges and tickets for negroes, each....................... 25
" affixing the seal of the City to any document for any person other than the City,... 50
" each subpœna for a witness,............................... 15

Should the defendant be discharged for want of proof, or his or her inability to pay costs, none of the fees in the ordinance shall be charged to the city.

POLICE.

Section 1. *Be it ordained, &c.* That the police force of the city shall consist of a Marshal and one or more Deputy Marshals, and six police-men. The Mayor shall appoint two of the police-men to act as lieutenants.

Sec. 2. The Marshal and Deputy Marshals shall be elected by the City Council, who shall have full power to dismiss said Marshal or Deputy Marshals from office, at any regular meeting of Council, for neglect of duty or mal-practice in office.

Sec. 3. The police-men shall be nominated by the Mayor and approved by the City Council; and such police-men may be removed from office by the Mayor, at any time, for incompetency, drunkenness, neglect of duty, mal-practice in office, or any misdemeanor.

Sec. 4. The principal Marshal elect shall, before entering upon the discharge of the duties of his office, give a bond, with two good securities, in the sum of two thousand dollars, payable to the Mayor and Council of the city of Macon, and conditioned for the faithful discharge of his duties as Marshal, and the proper application of all funds which shall come into his hands as such officer. The Deputy Marshals shall, in like manner, give bonds in the sum of one thousand dollars, each, which bonds shall be increased or strengthened as Council may direct.

Sec. 5. The principal Marshal and each Deputy Marshal shall be vested with full power and authority to serve all processes, executions, attachments and rules of the Mayor and Council of the City of Macon, for which service they shall, in addition to their salary receive the following fees:

For collecting tax execution without levy,........................	$	35
" executing warrant or levy, and return of execution,............		1 00
" attending trial before the Mayor, of a white person,............		50
" attending trial before the Mayor, of a negro,.................		25
" arrest of a white person,..................................		1 25
" arrest of a negro,....		50
" serving subpœnas, each,.............................		31¼
" whipping a negro when ordered by the owner,...............		1 00

Should the defendant be discharged for want of proof, or his or her inability to pay costs, none of the fees in this ordinance shall be chargable to the city.

Sec. 6. It shall be the duty of the principal Marshal to attend all meetings of the Council, and preserve order: also, to visit the Reserve, daily, to prevent trespass thereon, and to prosecute all violations of the ordinances of the city, in relation thereto.

Sec. 7. It shall be the duty of the Marshal and Deputy Marshals to enforce and carry into effect, to the utmost of their power, all the ordinances of the city, in force; to obey and execute all the commands and orders of Council, as well as those of the Mayor or any member of Council, in relation to any matter or thing affecting the interests of the city.

Sec. 8. It shall be the duty of the Marshal and Deputy Marshals to collect all executions for taxes or fines, placed in their hands by the Clerk and Treasurer, as also all money received for slaves and public exhibitions; and shall pay over the same to the Treasurer when required; and upon failure to pay over moneys when collected, after demanded by the Treasurer, he or they shall forfeit and pay to the City the sum of ten dollars for each and every day the said moneys are retained, together with the interest on the sum in his or their hands, until paid.

Sec. 9. It shall be the duty of the Marshal, Deputy Marshals, and the Police-men to preserve order in the city; to arrest all drunken, disorderly or riotous persons who are disturbing the peace and quiet of the city; also to patrol the city at night, to disperse all illegal assemblages of negroes, and to take up all negroes found violating the laws of the city, or who may be away from the premises of their owner or employer after the hour designated by Council for the ringing of the Guard House Bell without a written permit, and to commit all such offenders to the Guard House or common Jail of Bibb county, there to remain until the next morning, when they shall be brought before the Mayor, there to be dealt with as the evidence produced shall warrant. And in case of their inability to suppress such disorders, or to disperse such riotous assemblages, they shall have power to call to their assistance a sufficient number of persons to act as additional Deputy Marshals for the occasion, and whose compensation shall be fixed by the Council.

SEC. 10. It shall be the duty of the Marshal, and all other police officers, to take all slaves or free persons of color to some retired place within the city, when necessary to whip, unless the punishment shall be ordered by the Mayor to be executed in a public manner, in which case the Guard House shall be the place designated.

SEC. 11. It shall be the duty of the Lieutenants to divide the Police-men in squads and assign them their respective posts, and to give them such instructions as he may from time to time receive from the Mayor or principal Marshal. They shall visit each post as often as practicable, and see that all are in the faithful performance of their duty. The Lieutenants shall report to the Marshal by 8 o'clock each morning all transactions of the police for the night previous, together with all infractions of the City Charter and Ordinances which may have come to their knowledge. The Marshal shall report the same to the Mayor each morning by 10 o'clock; and he shall, at the same time, ascertain from the Mayor if there be any orders to execute.

SEC. 12. The police-men selected to be on duty the first part of the night shall report themselves at 6 o'clock, P. M. They shall remain on duty until 12 o'clock at night, when they shall report themselves to the Lieutenants. Those appointed to do duty the latter part of the night, shall report themselves at the Guard House 15 minutes before 12 o'clock at night, to take the posts assigned them. They shall remain on duty until 6 o'clock, A. M.

SEC. 13. The Lieutenants shall keep a book in which they shall enter the name of every police-man found, or reported to be, absent from his post or derelict in duty; and no member of of the police force shall receive pay for such time as he shall be found absent from his post, or neglecting his duty.

SEC. 14. The whole police force shall be subject to the call of the Marshal, when the necessities of official duty demand it. Any person who shall molest or interfere with the Marshal, Deputy Marshals or police officers of the city whilst acting as patrols in the city of Macon, or shall by carrying away, secreting or by any other means prevent the arrest of any slave or slaves found out at night in violation of the ordinances relative to slaves, such person shall be fined by the Mayor of said city in a sum not exceeding one hundred dollars, or imprisoned in the common Jail of Bibb county, or in the Guard House of said. city for a space not more than one month, at the discretion of. the Mayor.

SPECIAL MARSHAL

SECTION 1. The Mayor and Council of the city of Macon will, on their first regular meeting, and annually thereafter, or whenever a vacancy occurs in said office, elect an additional Marshal. The candidate to be so elected, to be first nominated by the Rail Road companies, which may be done in writing under the hands of any two or more of the general superintendents and presidents of said Rail Road companies, to be known and called the Special Marshal; whose duty it shall be to attend and wait at the Rail Road Passenger Depot at all suitable, proper and necessary times as may be directed by written order to him addressed, signed by any two or more of said general superintendents and presidents; to preserve good order and the public peace. It shall be his duty to suppress in and about said Depot, all riotous and disorderly conduct, and to bring all persons who may in any manner disturb the public peace before the Mayor and Council for trial.

SEC. 2. The compensation of said Marshal shall be one thousand dollars per annum, payable quarterly, and the same shall be paid by the Rail Road companies owning said Depot, to whom alone the said Marshal shall look for payment of his salary, and the said Marshal will be dismissed and deposed from said office of Special Marshal at any time on the petition of said Rail Road companies—provided the petition be signed by all of the superintendents, and two of the presidents of said Rail Road companies.

SEC. 3. The office of Special Marshal will, at any time, be abolished by Council or a new appointment made at the request of the Rail Road companies.

RIOTOUS AND DISORDERLY PERSONS.

SECTION 1. The Mayor shall be authorized, at his discretion, to impose a fine not exceeding the sum of one hundred dollars, or imprisonment in the Guard House for thirty days, or both, on any person or persons who shall have been convicted before him of disorderly or riotous conduct, of assault and battery not amounting in law to felony, of affrays or fighting, or malicious mischief, whether in public or private places within his jurisdiction.

SEC. 2. It shall be the duty of the Marshal, Deputy Marshals and regularly appointed police of the city, to use all proper diligence in the arrest of any person or persons accused as aforesaid, summon the witnesses in a legal manner, bring them before the Mayor and enforce his decisions without unnecessary delay.

SEC. 3. In all cases in which the penalty for the violation of the laws of the State within the jurisdiction of the Mayor is not specified in the ordinances of the city, it shall and may be lawful for the Mayor to impose a fine at his discretion not exceeding one hundred dollars, or imprisonment in the Guard House, or both as aforesaid, if a white person: if a negro or free person of color, by fine or corporeal punishment, at his discretion, not to exceed thirty-nine lashes on any one day.

GUARD HOUSE, FEES, &c.

SECTION 1. From and after the passage of this Ordinance, it shall be the duty of the Guard House Keeper to confine persons imprisoned by the Ordinances of the said city, or otherwise, in separate apartments, one of which being allowed for males, the other for females.

SEC. 2. The Guard House Keeper shall demand and receive from the owner of every slave, and from every person of color, committed to the Guard House, the undermentioned sums for the following items of charges :

For receiving a prisoner,		$ 60
"	discharging a prisoner,	60
"	dieting a white person, per day,	50
"	dieting a negro, per day	30
"	whipping a negro by order of the owner or the Mayor,	50
"	whipping a negro (runaway).	1 00

If a slave should, in case of sickness, require further or better diet, on the recommendation of the Physician attending such slave, the cost of such extra diet, which shall be proved by producing the written recommendation of the Physician and the bill for the articles furnished.

For the Medicines and attendance bestowed on a sick slave, the amount of the Physician's bill for the same.

For advertising a fugitive slave, the amount of the Printer's bill for the same.

If a slave is kept at the Guard House for two weeks, the Guard House Keeper shall demand and receive from his or her owner, full payment of fees, charges and expenses due to the end of the said term, for and on account of such slave, and in like manner at the end of every two weeks.

SEC. 3. The fees for fugitive slaves committed at the Guard House, shall in all cases be the same as imposed by the laws of the State of Georgia.

SEC. 4. The Guard House Keeper shall discharge no slave or free person of color until the above fees, charges and expenses for such slave or free person of color shall be paid, and he shall be charged in the monthly settlement of the account with the fees, charges and expenses due for every slave or free person of color discharged by him within the preceding month.

SEC. 5. One-half of all fees (excepting that for dieting and whipping) shall be payable to the city, the other half to the Guard House Keeper: and should the defendant be discharged for want of proof, or his or her inability to pay costs, none of the fees in the Ordinance shall be chargable to the city, except that of the Guard House Keeper for dieting.

SEC. 6. It shall be the duty of the Guard House Keeper to keep a regular book showing all persons confined, for what committed, also showing when discharged, and by whose authority discharged, and he shall render to the Mayor and Aldermen at each regular meeting, an account of all persons received and discharged, with the names of the owners of each slave, and also of all moneys collected and disbursed for the week preceding— which weekly return shall be filed by the Clerk. It shall also be his duty to pay over monthly to the Treasurer the city's quota of all moneys collected, the amount of which shall be regularly reported by the Clerk to Council, and on failure or neglect of the Guard House Keeper to settle as aforesaid, it shall be the duty of the Clerk to report said failure or neglect to the Mayor and Council.

SEC. 7. The Guard House Keeper shall be authorised to make special contracts under the approval of the Mayor, when gangs of negroes are introduced.

Passed August 25, 1854.

GUARD HOUSE KEEPER.

Council shall elect, at the first regular meeting in each year, a Keeper of the Guard House, whose duty it shall be to remain constantly at the Guard House, and receive all prisoners from the officers, entering in a book to be kept for that purpose, the name of the prisoner, for what cause committed, and by whom arrested, together with the time of their discharge, and by what authority discharged. He shall receive all fees, and make a full return to the City Treasurer each week, (to be laid before Council) and pay over the amount due the city; he shall give bond with two securities for $1,000, conditioned for the faithful performance of his duty. He shall, in addition to his other duties, keep the Guard House and cells in a neat and cleanly order. He shall receive for his services such compensation as shall annually be fixed by Council, and have the exclusive privilege of boarding prisoners and receiving such fees for so doing as fixed by Council, and shall have the use of the Guard House lot. He may be removed from office at any regular meeting of Council. . No slave or free person of color shall be discharged from the Guard House except on the order of the Mayor or of the owner or Guardian of such slave or free person of color after paying all fees and fines.

Passed February 6, 1855.

SECTION 1. The Clerk of the Market, elected by Council, shall at the meeting next ensuing his election, give bond, conditioned for the faithful performance of his duty, with security, to be approved by Council, in the sum of five hundred dollars. He shall attend at the Market-house every day during market-hours, and shall enforce all rules and regulations of the market, to prevent the sale of diseased, stale, or unwholesome articles, and shall see that all weights and measures used in the Market correspond with the standard authorized by the laws of the State.

SEC. 2. In case of sickness or inability of the Clerk of the Market to attend at the Market-house, he shall employ a deputy Clerk, for whose acts he shall be responsible.

SEC. 3. It shall be the duty of the Clerk of the Market to superintend the Market, to preserve order and cleanliness; and to have the Market swept, and the stalls, blocks, and benches, cleaned daily, after the market hours are over. And he shall regulate the manner of arranging carriages and carts of persons bringing provisions to market.

SEC. 4. The Market fees shall be as follows :

For each beef brought to Market,	$ 30
For each quarter of beef, when less than a whole carcass is brought to market,	10
For each hog, when weighing less than twenty pounds,	5
For each hog, weighing between twenty and seventy-five pounds,	10
For each hog weighing over seventy five pounds,	20
For each sheep brought to Market,	20
For each goat brought to Market,	10

The Clerk of the Market shall be authorized to demand said fees in advance, and in case of refusal, the person so refusing shall be expelled the Market.

SEC. 5. It shall be the duty of the Clerk of the Market to require all persons bringing any cattle, sheep, hogs, or goats to Market, to furnish a description of the color, brands, and marks of the animals, and to produce the ears, which description, brand, mark, etc., it shall be the duty of the Clerk of the Market to record in a book kept by him for that purpose, subject to the inspection of any person, on the payment of a fee of ten cents.

SEC. 6. It shall be the duty of the Clerk of the Market to collect the fees established by said (fourth) section, and to keep a regular book thereof; and report the same to the City Council weekly, which sum when so reported, shall be paid over to the Treasurer of said City Council.

For the services of said officer, the City Council shall establish a salary as in case of the other officers elected.

5

BRIDGE KEEPER.

Section 1. The Bridge Keeper elected by the Council, shall give bond with two or more good securities, in the sum of two thousand dollars. He shall, at the first meeting after his election, submit to the Council, for their approval or disapproval, the name of his assistant, for whose acts he shall be responsible. He shall report weekly the amount of toll received by him, and shall pay the same to the Treasurer. His report shall be made up on the morning of the day on which the regular meeting of the Council is held, and for every failure to report, he shall forfeit and pay the sum of ten dollars. And if he shall at any time fail to make such report, and pay over the amount of toll in his hands, after notice, he may be dismissed from his office, and the Council shall fill the vacancy as they may deem expedient.

Sec. 2. It shall be the duty of the Bridge Keeper to place on a post at each end of the Bridge, in large letters, the rates of toll, and the prohibition to any person to pass the bridge faster than in a walk. He shall keep three lamps suspended in the interior of the Bridge, at suitable distances, and shall keep the same lighted and burning from night-fall to ten o'clock at night. And for every breach of these duties, he shall be subject to the penalty of ten dollars. He shall sweep the Bridge daily, and remove the dirt and filth that may accumulate upon it. He shall also report to Council from time to time, such repairs as may be necessary to the Bridge.

Sec. 3. The Bridge Keeper shall report the rates of toll established by the following section, except in cases otherwise ordered by Council. It shall be his duty to preserve the Bridge from injury, or being damaged, and he shall report all persons injuring or defacing the same, to the Marshal, to be by him prosecuted for malicious mischief.

Sec. 4. The following shall be the rates of Toll on and over said Bridge, to wit:

4 wheel Carriage		with 4 horses, shall pay				60 cents.
4	"	"	" 2	"	"	50
4	" Barouche	" 4	"	"		60
4	" "	" 2	"	"		50
4	" "	" 1	"	"		35
4	" Rockaway	" 2	"	"		50
4	" "	" 1	"	"		35
3	" Pedlar's wagon, 2 horses, shall pay, with or without springs,					35
4	" " " 1	"	"	"	"	25
Gig or Sulkey, with 1	"	"	"	"	"	26
Man and horse						5
Road wagon, 6 horses						45
" " 5 "						40

Road wagon, 4 horses.................................... 35 cents.
" " 3 " 30
" " 2 " 25
Cart with 1 horse............................. 10
Ox Carts and wagons, the same rates as drawn by horses,. 3
Stock Cattle, Hogs, Sheep and Goats, each. 2

SEC. 5. Any person or persons crossing the Macon Bridge in carriages or vehicles of any description, or on horseback, in a faster gait than a walk, shall, on conviction before the Mayor, be fined in a sum not less than five nor more than ten dollars, at the discretion of the Mayor.

THE SEXTON.

SECTION 1. At the first meeting of Council after his election, the Sexton shall give bond in the sum of five hundred dollars, for the faithful discharge of his duties, with security, to be approved by Council. It shall be his duty to superintend the digging of all graves, and all interments made in the burying grounds of the city. He shall dig all graves to the depth of five feet, and shall see that no person is buried in any place within the corporate limits of the city, other than the Cemeteries of the City.

SEC. 2. He shall keep a book of record of all deaths and burials in the city, mentioning the names, age, place of nativity, disease, residence, in which Cemetery buried, and submit the same monthly to the Council.

SEC. 3. The Sexton shall be entitled to the following fees, viz.:

For digging a grave, and making interment of a white person, $4 00
For digging a grave, and making interment of a negro, . . . 3 00
For walling up a grave with good hard brick and lime mortar, where less than five hundred are used, two dollars a hundred, . . . 2 00
Where more than five hundred are used, one dollar and fifty cents per hundred, ... 1 50
In cases where parties furnish their own brick and material, he shall receive for laying the same fifty cents per hundred, . . . 50
Where parties furnish their own material and labor, in walling up graves,, the Sexton shall only be entitled to his regular fee of . 4 00
For digging a grave of more than seven and a half feet in length, for a white person, ... 5 00

And he may demand his fees for all burials in advance, from persons living without the limits of the city.

SEC. 4. The Sexton shall take charge of the City Burial Ground, and keep the buildings, fences, and other appurtenances thereto belonging in proper order and condition; shall be always ready to receive verbal or written applications for interments on the said ground, and to make, without delay, all interments for which he may be applied to as aforesaid.

Sec. 5. Any person making application to the Sexton for the interment of any person, in the aforesaid city burial ground, who died beyond the limits of the city of Macon, shall pay to him, besides his own fees, and at the time of paying such fees, five dollars for the use of the city, and which sum so received he shall pay over to the City Treasurer every three months. He shall keep a cash book, in which he shall, from day to day, enter all sums thus received for the city, as well as all fees and perquisites by him received, and cast up at the end of every month the aggregate amount by him collected and received as aforesaid.

Sec. 6. The Sexton shall bury all paupers, when so directed by the Mayor, or any member of Council, and be entitled to such fee therefor as may be fixed by Council.

Sec. 7. If the Sexton shall exact more than the fees herein before authorized, he shall be removed from his office. And for any failure or refusal to dig a grave within six hours after being notified so to do, or for any other failure or neglect properly to discharge the duties of his office, he shall be fined in a sum not less than twenty dollars, or removed from office at the discretion of Council.

CITY SURVEYOR.

Section 1. It shall be his duty, on the application of the City Council, or of any citizen, to repair to any place within the city, and there designate and define the boundary of any lot or lots, street or streets; and for such service so rendered by said surveyor, he shall receive from the person or persons employing him, five dollars for the survey of each lot, and making out a plot and certificate of the same.

Sec. 2. Before entering upon the discharge of his duties, the City Surveyor shall take and subscribe the following oath, viz.:

I, A. B., do solemnly swear, (or affirm, as the case may be) that I will to the best of my knowledge and skill, and without any favor or affection to any party, correctly survey any lot or lots, or streets, when called upon for that purpose, so help me God.

MAYOR, PRO TEM.

The said Mayor and Council shall, at their first meeting in each and every year, elect from their body a Mayor *pro tem.*, who shall be clothed with all the rights, privileges, and duties of the Mayor elect, and who shall act as such during the illness or absence from any cause of said Mayor, having first taken the usual oath of office, and not otherwise; and if the said Mayor elect or Mayor *pro tem.*, should both be unable from any cause to attend to their duties, the Council shall elect another Mayor *pro tem.*

from their body, who shall be clothed with all the rights, privileges and duties of the said Mayor, upon taking the said oath of office, and who shall only act as such in the absence of the said Mayor elect or Mayor *pro tem.* aforesaid.

BOARD OF HEALTH.

SECTION 1. The City Council at its first meeting in the month of April, shall appoint a Board of Health, to consist of nine citizens, five of whom shall be a quorum, and who shall meet once a week, or as often as they may deem necessary. It shall be the duty of the Board of Health, to visit and examine every part of the city, with a view to ferret out and detect all causes of disease that may endanger the health of the city, or any neighborhood thereof.

SEC. 2. The Board of Health shall report to Council the existence of any standing water, filth, impure or rotten fruit, together with all causes of disease and nuisances that may injuriously affect the health of the city. And it shall be the duty of Council to act promptly upon all reports of the Board of Health so made, by carrying out their recommendations, and causing the nuisances and inducements to disease to be abated and removed, at the expense of the person or persons by whose negligence or agency they are produced, or of the owner of the premises on which they are found to exist.

SEC. 3. The Board of Health shall report to Council all lots and cellars in which water may stagnate, or which from their location may be liable to become the seat of such nuisance, or other causes of disease, and upon such report, the City Council shall forthwith require the owner of such lot to fill up or drain the same, so as effectually to remove or abate the nuisance complained of, and the owner or occupant of such cellar, also to have the same baled and kept dry; and in case of refusal by such owner or occupant to comply with the requirements of Council, in a reasonable time, the Council shall have the same done at their expense, in the manner pointed out and directed in the twenty-second section of the Charter of the city.

SEC. 4. The Board of Health shall advise the City Council of any danger at any time, of the introduction into the city of the small pox, or other malignant disease or epidemic, and recommend measures for the prevention thereof, and for the most speedy relief of the city from such visitations, when they have made their appearance.

SEC. 5. The Board of Health shall be organized by the election of a chairman, who shall preside at all meetings thereof, and direct the Clerk to report all the proceedings of the body to the Council. They may adopt such by-laws, rules and regulations, not inconsistent with the Charter of the city, as they deem pro-

per, and do all other acts and things not specified in this ordinance, that will promote and secure the health of the city.

MARKET.

SECTION 1. Each day of the week (Sundays excepted) shall be
a public market day, and the public market shall be held at the
Market House, and at no other place.

SEC. 2. The Market Bell shall be rung fifteen minutes before
sun rise all seasons of the year, and the market hours shall from
thence continue until ten o'clock, A. M., during the months of
October, November, December, January, February and March,
and until nine o'clock, A. M., during the months of April, May,
June, July, August and September, in each year, except on Saturday, when there shall be an extra market in the afternoon, from
four to nine o'clock in the Fall and Winter months; and from
five to ten o'clock in the Spring and Summer months.

SEC. 3. Any person or persons who shall sell, or offer for sale
during Market hours, any fresh Meats, Poultry. Game or Wild
Fowls, Eggs, Butter, fresh Fish, Fruits, Vegetables or Provisions of any kind, usually brought to market, in any of the streets
of the city other than at the Market House, such person or persons violating this section shall pay a fine not exceeding ten dollars; and if by a slave, or free person of color, shall be punished
by whipping, at the discretion of the Mayor.

SEC. 4. The stalls in the Market House shall be rented out to
the highest bidder, under the direction of the committee on the
market, during the month of January in each year: there shall
be reserved two stalls, and such other places as said committee
may direct, for the use of persons sending or bringing meat of
their own stock to market. No person shall have a right to dispose of, or transfer his stall without the consent of the committee,
and no one person or company of persons shall be permitted to
rent more stalls than one, until all applicants are supplied, of
which the committee alone shall be the judges.

SEC. 5. It shall be the duty of persons renting stalls for the
purpose of vending meats, to keep blocks or benches for cutting
up the same, and to see that they are preserved free from all rot
or decay, or from the accumulation of dirt, filth, or trash, under
a penalty of five dollars for each offence.

SEC. 6. All persons bringing vegetables, poultry, or other provisions to market, shall have assigned to them by the Clerk, free
of charge, a stand which they have the exclusive right of using,
for the time being, and no person shall be allowed any other
stand than the one assigned him; *Provided*, That persons bringing poultry, butter and eggs to market, shall be permitted, under
the direction of the Clerk of the Market, to sell the same from

their carts, wagons, or other vehicles, at and around the Market House, without charge.

SEC. 7. It shall not be lawful for any person or persons to purchase during Market hours, any thing offered for sale at the Market, for the purpose of offering the same for sale in the city or market. Any person or persons violating this Ordinance shall be fined not more than fifty, nor less than twenty dollars, for each and every such offence:—one half of said fine to go to the informer, and the other half to the City Treasury.

SEC. 8. A fine of not more than twenty dollars shall be inflicted on every white person who may be convicted before the Mayor's Court for selling, or offering or attempting to sell at or near the public Market, any meat, fish or poultry, game or wild fowl, eggs, vegetables, fruit, butter, or any other article or commodity, or provisions of any kind usually brought to market for sale, and which said person may have bought at or near said Market at any time less than one week before: and the penalty of not less than thirty lashes shall be inflicted on any slave or free person of color convicted before the Mayor's Court of a violation of any of the foregoing provisions as defined in the case of a free person.

SEC. 9. It shall be the special duty of the Clerk of the Market and of the City Police to report all violations of said Ordinance, (section 9), and to put the offender or offenders on the Information Docket; and in every case where the offender is not a resident of the city, it shall be the duty of said Clerk or Police to seize every such article or commodity, and detain the same, until the offender shall answer for said offence before the Mayor's Court.

SEC. 10. It shall not be lawful for any person to smoke any cigar or pipe in the public Market House of the City of Macon, under a penalty of two dollars for the first offence, and not exceeding five dollars for each and every subsequent offence, if the offender be a white person, and under a penalty not exceeding three dollars, or whipping, not exceeding ten lashes, if a slave or free person of color.

SEC. 11. If any person shall cut, mutilate, break or deface, or injure the Market building or stalls, or other appurtenances to the said Market building, such offender shall be fined in a sum not exceeding fifty dollars, one half of the fine to be paid to the informer.

SEC. 12. No dog shall be permitted to come within the Market building during market hours; and any person or persons bringing a dog or dogs with him or her, contrary to the provisions of this section shall be fined in a sum not exceeding ten dollars.

SEC. 13. It shall not be lawful for any person or persons to sleep or lie down upon any of the public stalls in the Market House in the night or day time; and every person so found shall be arrested by the Marshal, or City Police, and upon conviction before the Mayor, shall be fined in a sum not exceeding five dollars.

SEC. 14. It shall not be lawful for any person or persons bringing any description of articles usually brought to the Market for sale, to keep any wagon, cart, or other vehicle, nearer to the Market building, or for a longer time, than any member of the Market Committee or the Clerk of the Market may direct, and such person or persons shall be compelled to take such position with their wagons, carts, or other vehicles, as said officers shall deem best for convenient sale, and the better protection of the interests of those who rent stalls within the enclosure of the Market building; and any person or persons refusing to conform to this regulation, shall, on conviction before the Mayor, be fined in a sum not exceeding ten dollars.

SEC. 15. It shall be the duty of the Clerk of the Market, from time to time, as he may think necessary, to examine the scales and weights of all buying or selling in the Market, and prescribe the manner of suspending their scales; and any person refusing to conform to such direction shall be fined in a sum not exceeding twenty dollars.

SEC. 16. It shall not be lawful for the butchers who have stalls in the Market building, or for any other person or persons whatever, to enter the enclosure with a wagon, cart, or other vehicle, or on horseback. Every person so offending shall pay a fine not less than five, nor more than ten dollars, on conviction before the Mayor.

SEC. 17. No person, except the owner or party in charge, shall mount upon any wagon, cart, or other vehicle at market without leave, and no person shall take from any individual at market any article whatever without permission of the owner, or without having paid for the same. Every white person so offending shall pay a fine not less than one nor more than ten dollars. If a slave or free person of color, shall be punished by whipping, at the discretion of the Mayor.

AN ORDINANCE

To prohibit slaves or free persons of color from trading in poultry, provisions, or other produce, or from trading or trafficking in any way whatever within the limits of the City of Macon.

SECTION 1. No slave or free person of color shall sell or offer for sale in or about the Market, during market hours, any kind of poultry, produce, or provisions of any description, without a written permit from his, her or their owner or owners, overseer, employer or guardian.

SEC. 2. No slave or free person of color shall be allowed to sell or offer for sale in the market or on the street, or in any shop, store, or other place, within the limits of the city, any poultry, produce, provisions, or any other chattel or other thing than those raised or produced by his, her or their owner or owners, employer or guardian, under no pass or pretext whatever.

Sec. 3. It shall be the duty of the Police or Clerk of Market to seize all articles so offered, and apprehend all slaves or free persons of color and bring him, her. or them before the Mayòr, who shall have the power to confiscate all such articles so offered. The officer so apprehending shall be entitled to one half of the proceeds of such articles so confiscated, the other half to go to the poor of the city.

ICE.

Section 1. It shall not be lawful for any person to sell Ice within the corporate limits of the City of Macon on the Sabbath day, only between the hours of 12, M., and 1, P. M. Any person violating this section, shall, on proof thereof, be fined by the Mayor of said city for each offence in a sum not less than ten nor more than thirty dollars. When the Mayor is satisfied from the production of physicians' certificates, or other perfectly satisfactory proof, that Ice has been sold at other times on the Sabbath than those above mentioned on account of sickness, he may remit the penalty.

Sec. 2. Nothing in the foregoing shall be so construed as to permit any person who keeps Ice for sale, to sell anything, or any other article on the Sabbath day, during the hours when he is allowed by said section to sell Ice.

SLAVES AND FREE PERSONS OF COLOR.

Section 1. It shall not be lawful for any person or persons to confine or chastise any slave or any free person of color in any street or alley of the city.

Sec. 2. Free negroes and free persons of color, arriving within this city, shall within thirty days after their arrival, pay to the Treasurer fifty dollars. In case of neglect or refusal to pay the same, every such person or persons shall be committed to the Guard House or common Jail of the county, until the same is paid, or he, she, or they be discharged by order of Council, or by due course of law. No free negro or free person of color shall remain within the limits of the city a longer time than five days, without giving notice of who is his or her guardian or protector, to the Clerk of the Council; and it shall be the duty of said guardian personally to acknowledge himself as such to the Clerk within the above specified time, and that he, the said guardian, will be bound to pay all taxes which may be imposed on said free negro, or free person of color, by Council; and will hold him or herself accountable for the good conduct and behavior of said

6

free negro or free person of color, the same as is regulated by law in regard to the relationship between master and slave; and it shall be the duty of the Clerk of Council to keep a book register of all free negroes and free persons of color, the date of register, their names, occupation, age, and name of guardian; and it shall be the duty of the Marshal to apprehend all free negroes, or free persons of color, who may violate and disregard the provisions of this section, and lodge them in the Guard House or Jail until released by the Mayor and City Council, to whom he shall report his acts and doings, at the first regular meeting of Council thereafter.

SEC. 3. No slave or slaves shall be permitted to live on lots detached from the residence of their owners or employers without a license from the Mayor and Council; and said slave or slaves when so licensed, shall be under the immediate supervision of the Police, who shall have full power to enter their dwellings whenever they may deem it necessary for the good order and safety of the city. No slave shall be allowed to hire his own time, or carry on any trade within the limits of this city, except that of a barber or hair dresser, or be engaged in any work or employment, except under the immediate control of his master or employer. No slave shall be hired to, or by any free person of color, (except it be done legally through the guardian of such free person of color,) or another slave directly or indirectly, at any time within the limits of this city, under a penalty of ten dollars for each and every such offence.

SEC. 4. No keeper or manager of a livery stable shall hire or loan to any slave, or free person of color, any horse, mule, carriage, or other conveyance whatever, without a written permit from the owner of such slave, or guardian of such free person of color, stating the place where he or she may be going, and the time of absence, under a penalty of five dollars for each violation of this Ordinance.

SEC. 5. Any slave or free person of color found after daylight down, or at any time on the Sabbath day, seen going in or coming out of any house, shop, or any other place in the city where liquors of any kind, wine, cider, beer or other spirituous or other fermented drinks are retailed or sold, unless sent by his or her master, employer or guardian, and have a written permit to that effect, such slave or free person of color shall be lodged in the Guard House and there kept until liberated by their master, employer or guardian on payment of the usual fee. And for the violation of this ordinance, the person or persons owning or keeping such house or shop, or other place, shall be fined in a sum not exceeding fifty nor less than ten dollars.

SEC. 6. No assemblage of negroes or people of color, in any part of the city, for the purpose of dancing or merriment shall take place without a written permit being first obtained from the

Mayor and any four members of Council, whose duty it shall be to prescribe the time when, and at what time to break up; and the Marshal and all other city officers are directed to enforce this Ordinance.

Sec. 7. No slave or free person of color shall buy any spirituous or fermented liquors, wine or cider, within the limits of the city, without a written permit from his or her master or guardian, and any liquors so bought may be seized and forfeited; and any person selling or giving spirituous liquors to a negro not his own, or free person of color, on conviction before the Mayor, shall be fined not exceeding one hundred dollars.

Sec. 8. No person shall employ or permit any negro or other slave, to sell for him any goods, wares or merchandize, or liquors, or other articles of any kind, unless the owner thereof, or another white person in the employ of such owner, be present; and every white person so offending, shall forfeit and pay the sum of twenty dollars for each and every such offence, with costs.

Sec. 9. No owner or other peson having the care or management of slaves, shall permit such slave to be hired or employed out of their respective families or houses, without obtaining from the City Clerk a ticket or badge, expressing the particular employment of said slave, and numbered, under the penalty of five dollars, with costs, for each offence. It shall be the duty of the Clerk to keep a book of record of said licenses granted, with particular description of the slave for whom the ticket is given.

Sec. 10. No person shall be allowed a badge or ticket for any slave but the owner, his or her agent, trustee, attorney or guardian.

Sec. 11. Badges or tickets shall not be transferable, and used by any other slave than the one for whom issued; a violation shall forfeit the badge or ticket, which shall not be renewed except by order of Council.

Sec. 12. It shall be the duty of the Marshal to seize all slaves found working without badges or tickets, and lodge them in the Guard House or Jail, who shall there remain, until liberated by their masters, or guardians, by paying five dollars and all costs.

Sec. 13. No assemblage of slaves or free persons of color, composed of more than seven in number, shall be permitted within the limits of this city, unless there be at least two white persons present, except when assembled at Church for religious worship, then the presence of one responsible white male resident shall be sufficient; and it shall be the duty of the Marshal, in all cases of violation, to disperse said assemblage of slaves, and free persons of color, and also arrest the leader or leaders of the same, and commit him or them to the Guard House, to be punished at the discretion of the Mayor.

Sec. 14. It shall be the duty of the Marshal and all other

Police officers, to take all slaves or free persons of color, to some retired place within the limits of the city, when necessary to whip or otherwise punish them, unless the punishment be ordered by the Mayor to be executed in a public manner, in which case the Guard House shall be the place of execution, between the hours of ten o'clock, A. M., and three o'clock, P. M.

Sec. 15. All negroes, slaves or free persons of color, being caught out from their owners' premises by the Marshal, Deputy Marshals, the City or Volunteer Police, after the ringing of the Guard House Bell at the hour P. M. established by Council, without a special permit from their owner, guardian or employer, shall be committed to the Guard House and there confined for the remainder of the night, and shall not be released by any officer of the city—under a penalty of not more than ten dollars for each and every offence—until regularly discharged the following morning in conformity with the Ordinance.

Sec. 16. When Council shall be advised at any time, that there is in the city a free person of color of notoriously bad or suspicious character, they shall notify such free person of color, through the Marshal or Deputy Marshals, to leave the city within five days, and in case of refusal or failure to do so, the Council shall cause said free person of color to be arrested and confined, until they can decide what action to take thereon, for the good of the city.

Sec. 17. In cases not specially provided for, if a slave or free person of color is charged with violating any part of an ordinance of the City Council, he or she may be tried by the Mayor or any two members of Council. If found guilty, the said Mayor or members may sentence the delinquent to receive a number of lashes not exceeding thirty-nine, within any one day, or be confined in the Guard House not more than five days, or both, at their discretion. Corporal punishment or confinement may be commuted for a pecuniary fine, not exceeding twenty dollars for such offence;—*Provided*, The master or guardian is willing to pay it.

Sec. 18. Slaves or free persons of color shall not assemble in, around or near, any street door, upon the side walk, or any other place or places to the annoyance of the neighbors or persons passing, nor to smoke in the streets, or alleys, or any public square or place. For a violation of this section, such negro or negroes shall be committed to the Guard House until the next morning, whipped and discharged, and the owner or occupant of the place or house shall be fined five dollars for each time he shall allow such assemblages of negroes.

It shall not be lawful for any slave, or any free person of color, on his or her own account, to sell or make Cotton Mattresses, or buy or sell Cotton for said purposes, under a penalty of twenty dollars, or to be punished at the discretion of the Mayor.

TRADING WITH SLAVES.

Any person who shall be guilty of trading or dealing with any slave or slaves, or of furnishing him, her or them with any spirituous or intoxicating liquors within the limits of the city of Macon, contrary to the laws of this State, shall, on proof thereof, before the Mayor, be fined by the Mayor of said city, in a sum of not more than one hundred dollars, or imprisoned in the common Jail of Bibb county, or Guard House of said city, not exceeding the space of one month,—or both fined and imprisoned, in the discretion of the said Mayor.

NEGRO GAMBLING.

Any slave or slaves, or free person of color, arrested by the Police, having about their persons cards, dice-box, or any other article known and used for gambling purposes, it shall be presumptive evidence that they have been, or intend gambling; and shall be punished at the discretion of the Mayor.

SLAVE MARTS.

Each and every person who shall keep and use within the limits of the City of Macon, any house, yard or other place for the purpose of keeping slaves therein for sale or hire, shall pay annually on the first day of January of each and every year, into the Treasury the sum of two hundred dollars: and if any person shall fail to comply with the requirements of this Ordinance, he or they shall be fined in a sum not exceeding one hundred dollars, and an execution shall issue for the whole sum and be collected in the usual manner.

MAGAZINE.

Section. 1. All gunpowder which shall be brought to the city for sale, on consignment, or for any purpose whatever, shall be conveyed by the owners or consignees thereof to the Magazine, within six hours after its arrival.

Sec. 2. No person shall keep for retail in their stores, more than fifty-six pounds of gunpowder, which shall be kept in a tin or copper canister. And any person offending against this provision, shall be liable to a fine of twenty dollars a day, for every day so offending, nor shall any person expose for sale any gunpowder in the streets or alleys of the city, under a similar penalty.

Sec. 3. All powder kept in the Magazine shall, when placed therein, be marked or labelled with the name of the owner or consignee, and all powder found in the streets, or any store, contrary to the provisions of this Ordinance, shall be seized by the Marshal or Deputy Marshals, and be by them conveyed to the Magazine, to await the order of Council, upon the report thereof by the officer seizing the same.

KEEPER OF THE MAGAZINE.

SECTION 1. The Keeper of the Magazine, elected by Council, shall, at the meeting next ensuing his election, give bond with good security, in the sum of one thousand dollars, conditioned for the faithful performance of his duty.

SEC. 2. It shall be the duty of the Keeper of the public Magazine, to attend at all times, when required, between sun rise and sun set, (Sundays excepted,) as well for the purpose of receiving, as delivering gunpowder to the owners thereof. He shall have a fixed place of residence or office, in some central part of the city, which he shall advertise. He shall receive all gunpowder, and enter the same in a book to the credit of the respective owners, issue receipts therefor, keep an account of, and report to Council monthly, the amount of gunpowder in the Magazine and the amount received for storage and the amount due. And it shall be, moreover, his duty, if any person storing gunpowder refuses or neglects to pay the storage due upon such portion as may not be removed in twelve months from the time of its receipt, after advertising in the public gazettes of the city for ten days, to sell such gunpowder at public auction, or so much thereof as will pay the amount of storage due. And in every instance, he shall receive the storage due on any gunpowder demanded of him, before its delivery.

SEC. 3. The Keeper of the Magazine shall receive for his services, the storage on gunpowder, which shall be at the following rates, to wit: one cent per pound for the first twelve months, or any part thereof, if paid by the owner in not exceeding ten days after the powder shall have been stored therein, and one and a half cents per pound if not so paid; and half a cent per pound for every six months following. A part thereof to be paid by the owner as the gunpowder is taken away, or sooner, at his option.

SEC. 4. It shall be the duty of the Keeper of the Magazine, to examine the building used for a Magazine from time to time, and report to Council any repairs which shall be necessary. And he shall examine monthly into the condition of all powder in the Magazine.

NUISANCES.

SECTION 1. It shall not be lawful for any person to build, have or keep any privy, nor dig, have or keep any sink or pit for a privy within four feet of any street or public alley, or within two feet of the boundary line of his or her own lot. And any person who shall be guilty of a violation of this section, shall be fined in a sum not exceeding twenty dollars for each day said nuisance shall continue after notice from the Mayor. And moreover, it shall be the duty of the Mayor and Council, in case of refusal by the owner or occupant of any lot on which such nuisance shall exist, to abate the same, and cause the Clerk to issue an execution against the offender for the amount expended.

Sec. 2. No person shall be allowed to build, have or keep any privy in the business parts of the city, without a pit or sink; and it shall be the duty of the Mayor and Council to remove any privy so erected, or kept, and to cause an execution to be issued against the owner of said lot for the amount so expended, after giving five days' notice to persons so offending; *Provided,* Any person may have under their privies, movable boxes or tubs, on condition that they are removed and cleansed once in every two weeks.

Sec. 3. No person shall be permitted to throw into the streets any rotten fruit, vegetables, dead carcasses or other matter, in such quantities as to become offensive, under a penalty of five dollars.

Sec. 4. No person shall kindle or build a fire in the streets of the city, nor shall any person be allowed to camp in the streets, under the penalty of ten dollars for every offence; *Provided,* that blacksmiths shall be allowed to build fires for the purpose of shrinking tires in front of their shops.

Sec. 5. It shall not be lawful for any person to fire a gun, pistol, or any other fire arms, within three hundred yards of any house, except in cases of military parade; nor shall any person burn rockets, crackers, or any kind of fire works within the limits of the city. Any person so offending shall be fined in a sum not exceeding twenty dollars.

Sec. 6. No person shall be permitted to fly a kite in any part of the city, and it shall be the duty of the Marshal and Deputy Marshals, in case of a violation of this Ordinance, to destroy the kites so used, and in case of resistance or repetition, the offenders shall be arrested and brought before the Council to be dealt with as they may direct.

Sec. 7. No person shall do, or cause to be done, any work within the limits of the city on the Sabbath day, unless it be a work of necessity or charity.

Sec. 8. Any person who shall be found in the streets drunk, or acting in a disorderly, riotous or tumultuous manner, or who shall be guilty of any act against the public safety, morality and decency, not herein specified, shall be arrested by the Marshal and confined in the Guard House, until such time as he can be brought before the Mayor, to be dealt with as he may think proper.

Sec. 9. All lots and cellars within the limits of the city, shall by their owners or occupants be kept in such condition as not to allow any water to stagnate, or otherwise become offensive, or any other nuisance to exist thereon; and for a violation of this section, shall be fined in a sum not exceeding ten dollars per day, for each day said nuisance exists, after notice from the Mayor or Marshal. And it shall moreover be the duty of the Mayor and Council, after the refusal or neglect of any owner or occupant of any lot on which such nuisance shall exist, to abate the same, and cause the Clerk to issue an execution against such offender, and the lot on which such nuisance may exist, for the amount expended in abating such nuisance.

Sec. 10. Any owner or occupant of a lot, who shall throw or discharge, or permit or allow to be thrown or discharged, from his or her premises, as much water or other liquid or thing of any kind whatever, as may put any part of any street or alley in bad order, or which may injure or damage any other lot in any way, or the occupants thereof, shall be fined by the Mayor or any two members of Council, not exceeding ten dollars a day and costs, for every day such nuisance shall exist, and the same shall be abated by order of the Mayor, or two members of Council, at the charge and expense of the person or persons causing or allowing the same.

Sec. 11. No owner or occupant of any lot, shall keep on his or her premises, any nuisance, to the annoyance of his or her neighbors. Any person so annoyed may apply to the Mayor or any two members of Council, who shall require, in writing, an abatement of such nuisance, in such time as he or they may think reasonable or proper. And if such nuisance is not abated by the time required, such offender or offenders shall be fined in a sum not exceeding ten dollars a day, for each day the same may continue, or imprisoned in the discretion of the Mayor or said two members of Council, and such nuisance shall be forthwith abated at the charge and expense of such person or persons so offending.

Sec. 12. It shall not be lawful for any person or persons to construct gutters or spouts to convey filth from their lots into any of the alleys or streets of the city, under a penalty for each and every offence of a sum not exceeding twenty, nor less than five dollars, at the discretion of the Mayor: and said gutter or spout shall be removed within ten days from notice; otherwise they will be removed by and under the direction of the Marshal, and the expense obtained from the property by the usual process.

ANIMALS RUNNING AT LARGE.

If any horse, mare, gelding, colt, mule, ox, cow or calf, or any other animal of like kind, shall be found at large in the city, whose appearance shall be offensive to the sight from its poverty, sickness or lameness, the same shall be removed by the Marshal or any other city officer from the limits of the city at the expense of the owner or owners thereof, to be adjudged by the Mayor, before whom the parties shall be cited to appear; and if any person shall resist or oppose an officer in the discharge of such duty they shall be subject to a fine of not less than five nor more than twenty dollars.

DOGS.

SECTION 1. From and after the first day of May, next, there shall be provided by the Treasurer of the city, a sufficient number of badges to be marked "C. M." and numbered from ONE upwards, and he shall furnish the owner or owners of any dog or dogs, who may apply for the same, with one or more of said badges, as may be required, said owner or owners paying to said Treasurer for the use of said city, one dollar for every such badge, or such amount as may be affixed by Council; and which badges shall protect all dogs wearing them from being killed. And all dogs found running at large in said city at any time after said first day of May next, except such as may wear badges as above provided, shall be liable to be killed by the City Marshal, or such city officer or officers as he may authorize and appoint for that purpose; and for every dog so killed there shall be paid to the officer killing the same by the City Treasurer, the sum of fifty cents.

SEC. 2. This Ordinance shall remain in force from the time it takes effect until regularly repealed.

Passed February 6, 1858.

HOGS.

SECTION 1. It shall not be lawful for the owners of Hogs to permit them to run at large within the corporate limits of the city, except on the east side of the Ocmulgee river.

SEC. 2. It shall be the duty of the Marshal or his assistants to take up and impound, in the City Pound, all Hogs found running at large within the corporate limits of the city, and there keep them—giving notice in one of the newspapers of the city of their being impounded. If identified and proven within *ten days* thereafter, the owner shall have the right to release them, on the payment of one dollar for each Hog, and twenty-five cents per day for feeding, and expenses for advertising.

SEC. 3. If, at the expiration of ten days, no owner comes forward to prove or identify said Hogs—it shall be the duty of the Marshal or his assistants to sell them at public auction, from the lot whereon they are impounded, on the morning next after the expiration of the said ten days, and pay the proceeds thereof into the City Treasury; the Treasurer paying the Marshal or his assistants, twenty-five per cent. on amount of nett sales, as compensation.

SEC. 4. It shall not be lawful for any slave or free person of color, living on lots detached from their owners, employers or guardians, to have or keep a hog or hogs in the city of Macon.

of their own property or the property of any other slave or free person of color. Any slave or free person of color, who shall violate this Ordinance, shall be fined five dollars, or be punished by whipping, at the discretion of the Mayor; and the hog or hogs so kept shall be forfeited to the city, and sold by the Marshal as provided for under section 3.

STREET LAMPS, ETC.

Any white person who shall be convicted before the Mayor or Mayor and Council, of breaking, injuring, or in any manner unlawfully interfering with any lantern, post, or other fixture or thing used for or necessary to the lighting of the streets, alleys, public or private buildings of said city with gas or other thing for giving light, shall be fined not less than five or more than twenty dollars, and imprisoned not exceeding ten days in addition to such fine.

Should a negro be convicted of the same offence, he shall be punished by the same fine as a white person, or by whipping, or by both fine and whipping, in the discretion of the Mayor or Mayor and Council.

LICENSES.

SECTION 1. No person shall run a dray, cart or other carriage of transportation for hire within the city, without a license from the City Council, under the regulation of the annual license Ordinance.

SEC. 2. All persons obtaining such license shall give a bond with approved security, payable to the Mayor and Council of the city of Macon, in the sum of five hundred dollars, conditioned to make good all damages sustained by the carelessness, or other improper conduct of the driver of the dray, which bond shall, upon request, be assigned to the party aggrieved by such misconduct.

SEC. 3. Every dray shall be numbered in the order in which it is licensed, and the Clerk shall furnish to the owner its proper number fairly painted on tin, receiving twenty-five cents for the same; and the owner shall have it attached to some conspicuous part of said dray. Every dray without its number, shall be considered unlicensed. Drivers of licensed drays shall not, between sun rise and sun set refuse to carry a load to or from any part of the city, without a sufficient excuse; complaint of which may be made to the Mayor, who shall order his arrest by the Marshal, and shall adjudge the case as he may deem just and proper, and may impose a penalty of a fine not exceeding the sum of ten dollars, or the forfeiture of his license, or both at discretion. The price of hauling a load to or from any part of the city, shall be thirty cents, where the weight does not exceed twelve hundred pounds, over that weight the driver may charge fifteen cents for every five hundred pounds. The price of hauling cotton shall be twelve and a half (12½) cents per bale; a load not to exceed six (6) bales.

SEC. 4. No license shall be granted to a slave or free person of color, under any circumstances or pretext whatever.

SEC. 5. All licensed drays, the owners of which conform to the regulations of this Ordinance, shall be permitted to pass or repass the bridge free of toll, on such terms and conditions as may be prescribed by the Council.

SEC. 6. No person shall retail spirituous or fermented liquors, wine, beer, cider, or other spirituous or fermented drinks in quantities less than one quart, within the limits of the City of Macon, without a license from the City Council, to be issued by the Treasurer, on the payment of the sum fixed by the annual license ordinance.

SEC. 7. Each person taking out license shall give bond, with good and approved security, in the sum of five hundred dollars, to the Mayor and Council, conditioned to keep a decent and orderly house; and shall moreover take and subscribe an oath before some officer authorized to administer oaths, not to sell or give liquor to slaves; and any person who, having obtained such license, shall fail to keep a decent and orderly house, or shall violate any of the provisions of this Ordinance, shall, on proof of such offence before the Mayor of said city, be fined by said Mayor in a sum not exceeding one hundred dollars, or imprisoned in the common Jail of Bibb county, or Guard House of said city, for the space of not more than one month, at the discretion of said Mayor.

SEC. 8. No person shall retail in more establishments than one, at the same time, under one license, nor shall any one be permitted to retail spirituous or fermented liquors in any street or alley.

SEC. 9. Any person shall be entitled to a tavern license upon application to the Clerk and Treasurer, and giving bond with approved security, in the sum of five hundred dollars to keep an orderly and decent house, with good and sufficient accomodation for travellers, their horses and attendants, during the time of their license, in the face of which it is to be expressed, that his, her or their bar room shall not be kept open on the Sabbath day, or Sabbath night, except for one hour only at each meal, and then to sell only to boarders, or travellers stopping with the person taking out the license, and the person taking out such license, shall pay to the Treasurer the sum fixed in the annual license ordinance. Any person or persons violating this section, shall, on proof before t e Mayor, be fined in a sum not exceeding one hundred dollars, or forfeit his or their license, or both, at the discretion of said Mayor.

Sec. 10. No person shall pursue the business of a vendue master, without taking out a license from the City Council, and paying therefor the sum fixed upon, in the annual license ordinance.

Sec. 11. It shall be the duty of the City Council each January, to enact a license ordinance for one year, specifying the rates, terms and conditions upon which license shall be granted to retailers, drays, vendue masters, venders of lottery tickes, nine or ten pin alleys, billiard tables, slaves working about the city, free persons of color, lumber and wood wagons crossing the bridge, physicians crossing the bridge, and for such other purposes as Council may deem proper.

Sec. 12. No person shall exhibit or perform in this city, any kind of equestrian exercise, rope dancing, concerts of music, fire works, slight of hand, or give other exhibitions or amusement for gain, without first obtaining a license from the Mayor, who shall fix the price thereof, at such rates as in his discretion may be reasonable and proper.

Sec. 13. All licenses shall be for one year and no longer, and shall expire on the 10th day of January in each year, except those of tavern keepers, vendue masters and venders of lottery tickets, which shall expire one year from date, and shall not be transferable. *Provided,* Council may grant to applicants who do not apply at the regular time, licenses for the remainder of the year, by paying therefor such sum as the Council may think proper, but in no case less than one half the annual license.

Sec. 14. If any person or persons enumerated in the license ordinance as subject to take out a license, shall fail to do so, and yet violate the ordinance, he or they shall be subject to the payment of a fine equal to the license violated, or more, at the discretion of the Mayor, for each and every conviction.

VENDUE MASTER.

Section 1. It shall not be lawful for any person whomsoever, not being a licensed Vendue Master, or Sheriff, Coroner or Constable in execution of lawful process, or an Executor, Administrator or Guardian in the due execution of their trusts, to hold any public vendue sales, or auction, whatsoever, or to expose for sale by himself at public outcry, any goods, chattels, wares, produce or merchandize within the limits of the City of Macon.

And if, after the passage of this Ordinance, any person, other than the person hereinbefore named, shall hold any public auction whatsoever within the limits of the City of Macon, or shall expose for sale, by himself, at public outcry within the limits of the city, any goods, chattels, wares, merchandize or produce whatsoever, such persons so acting or so offending shall be subject and liable to a fine, for each and every offence, not exceeding fifty dollars, to be imposed and recovered on information before the Mayor of the city.

SEC. 2. When an application for the office of Vendue Master shall hereafter be made, the applicant shall set forth the store or place at which he intends to carry on the Vendue or Auction business; and no Auctioneer shall be permitted to hold, carry on or conduct any general Auction or Vendue business at any other store or house than the store or place so set forth, unless by special permission of Council; and hereafter, all license shall specify the store or place as set forth by the applicant, and such license shall not be in any way assignable;—*Provided*, always, that such license shall not prevent said Vendue Master from holding special Auction sales at any point within the city—and at any time during the continuance of said license—for the purpose of selling any goods, wares, merchandize, furniture or any other property: such sales to be made by said Vendue Master in good faith, and not with the intent to defraud the city.

SEC. 3. No Vendue Master shall hereafter be permitted to use his license in such manner as to allow any person, other than such Vendue Master to have part or share of the commissions or profits which may be made on the sales of such Vendue Masters. *Provided*. That if there may be two or more partners, and license be granted to *one* partner, the license shall set forth the name or names of the other partner or partners, who may be allowed to receive a share of such profits; and if any licensed Vendue Master shall use his license so that any person other than the person or persons named in the license shall receive a part or share of the commissions or profits on his sales, such Vendue Master shall be liable to a fine of fifty dollars, to be recovered on information before the Mayor of the city; and if any licensed Vendue Master shall carry on any general Auction at public outcry, at any place other than at the place named in his license, without special permisssion of Council, he shall be liable to a fine of fifty dollars, to be recovered on information before the Mayor of the city.

SEC. 4. The rates of taxes on sales at Auction, in this city, shall be as follows, to wit: on gross amount of sales when the sum shall not exceed one thousand dollars, one per centum; when the same shall exceed one thousand dollars, one half of one per centum; and all sales of real estate, negroes, and Bank or other stocks, one-fourth of one per centum: and all Vendue Masters or Auctioneers shall make their returns on oath on the first Monday in April, July, October and January in every year, of the amount of their sales at Vendue or Auction for the three months next preceding the time of their returns.

SEC. 5. Each Vendue Master or Auctioneer shall, previously to receiving their license, give a bond with approved security, to the Mayor and Council, in the sum of one thousand dollars, con-

54 ORDINANCES.

ditioned for the punctual payment of their taxes, and the faithful discharge of all the duties required of them by the ordinances of the city; and upon any neglect or refusal to make said returns, as before described, or to pay within ten days all sums due by him to the City Council, the Treasurer shall immediately put the bond of such Vendue Master in suit; and any Vendue Master so offending shall forfeit his said license.

ITINERANT TRADERS.

Section 1. It shall not be lawful for itinerant traders and dealers in corn, bacon, lard, flour, tobacco, and other articles of produce, or merchandize of any description, to sell or offer for sale said articles temporarily deposited, or held on deposit, at the Rail Road depots, or other places in said city for sale, unless the vendors thereof shall return the market value thereof to the Clerk of Council under oath, and pay to the said Clerk one-half of one per cent. upon the market value of said goods, so held on deposit aforesaid.

Sec. 2. In the event that any person or persons shall violate the above Ordinance, it shall be the duty of the Marshal or Marshals of said city, to seize the said goods, and bring the offenders before the Mayor of said city, who upon ascertaining the market value thereof, shall require the Clerk of Council to issue executions against said offenders for one-half of one per cent. upon the market value of said goods so held on deposit aforesaid, which shall be levied upon the same by the Marshal aforesaid and sufficient thereof sold to satisfy the tax aforesaid.

Sec. 3. Said offenders shall be fined for said violation at the discretion of said Mayor, not exceeding the sum of fifty dollars for each violation.

STREETS, ALLEYS, AND SIDEWALKS.

Section 1. No streets or alleys shall be laid out, closed or altered, without the consent of three-fourths of the members of the City Council, and any person intending to make such application, shall give at least thirty days' notice thereof, in each of the gazettes of the city, and no such application shall be acted on, except at a regular meeting of the Council.

Sec. 2. No person shall be allowed to haul or dig any dirt, from any of the streets, commons, alleys, or reserve of the city, without the written permission of the Mayor, and at least two members of the Council; any violation shall be punished on conviction before the Mayor. If a negro, the punishment shall be whipping by the Marshal; if a white person, by a fine of five dollars a day for each day the same may continue.

Sec. 3. No person shall place in any street or sidewalk, any empty boxes or casks, or other obstructions of any kind. No person shall drive a dray, wagon or carriage of any kind nor ride a horse in the streets in a disorderly manner, so as to endanger other passengers. Nor shall any one drive, ride, or place any horse or mule, or any kind of carriage, on any sidewalk, or in any street or alley which intersects any walk in such a manner as to prevent the free passage of persons on foot, under the penalty of five dollars for the first, and ten dollars for the second offence.

Sec. 4. The sidewalks on the wide streets shall be twenty feet, those on the alternate narrow streets shall be sixteen feet wide, and those on Cotton Avenue shall be thirteen feet wide; and all trees and awning posts, on the several streets, shall be so set as to conform to this regulation, and shall be placed in a row. In case of deviation, it shall be the duty of the Council, after notice to the party so offending, and in case of refusal, to have such posts or trees removed.

Sec. 5. No person shall, without permission from the Council, erect any wooden shed or awning before his store or dwelling. Such permission shall not be given unless the party making the application shall have the awning erected by him neatly finished, painted, and with posts corresponding in length with those on the same street. *And provided*, That this permission shall not give to the party any right to the ground occupied by such shed, and may be withdrawn at any time. And any person fastening any horse or other animal, to any tree or box around it, or in any other way injuring the same, shall, on conviction of the same before the Mayor, be fined in a sum not less than five nor more than twenty dollars.

Sec. 6. It shall be lawful for any person, and the duty of the Marshals of the city, to take up any horse or mule found loose in the streets of the city, and forthwith summon the owner to appear before the Mayor, who may impose a fine for the offence at his discretion, not to exceed twenty dollars. In case the owner of any horse or mule taken up cannot be found, they shall be put in some lot or stable to be designated by the Mayor for safe keeping, and posted in one of the city papers, and if not claimed within ten days, shall be sold on the public square to pay the keeping and all costs. The Marshal's fee for taking up a loose horse or mule shall be one dollar, and for selling one dollar; to be paid by the owner, or from the sale of the same.

Sec. 7. That one dollar be charged for every horse or mule sold in the city by any drover or person bringing horses or mules and selling them in said city; and that the livery stable keepers be held responsible for one dollar per head for every horse or mule sold from their respective stables.

STREET ENCROACHMENT.

SECTION 1. No person shall be allowed to erect a fence, steps, portico or other obstruction beyond the line of their lots so as to be an encroachment upon the streets without first obtaining the consent of the Council.

SEC. 2. An I any person who shall so encroach upon any of the streets or alleys of the city, and on being notified to do so, shall neglect or refuse to remove said encroachment, shall be fined in a sum not exceeding five dollars for each and every day said encroachment may remain unremoved after such notice given.

SEC. 3. All encroachments hereafter made shall be equally liable to the provisions of this Ordinance, and shall be removed unless upon application to Council the same be permitted to remain.

SEC. 4. In all cases of encroachment upon streets, lanes or alleys in said city, the Mayor and Council may cause the same to be removed upon reasonable notice to the party causing the same, or, should they in their discretion deem it best, may permit and sanction the same, for such fair consideration as the parties may agree upon, due regard being first had to the interests of property holders likely to be affected thereby.

SEC. 5. All streets heretofore known and laid down in the original survey as wide streets, being one hundred and eighty (180) feet, shall from the passage of this Ordinance be only one hundred and thirty (130) feet wide; and all streets known and laid down in the original survey as narrow streets, being one hundred and twenty (120) feet, shall from the passage of this Ordinance be ninety (90) feet wide.

SEC. 6. The above shall not apply to that portion of the city lying between, and including Plum and Wharf streets, and Spring and Fifth streets; but the width of these streets shall remain as in the original survey; viz., one hundred and eighty (180) and one hundred and twenty (120) feet alternately; any encroachments within these limits must be by special permission of Council.

SEC. 7. That all property holders in the city, who avail themselves of the provisions of this Ordinance, be required to build their fences on an uniform line; that is, in all the wide streets, to build their fences sixty-five (65) feet, and in the narrow streets forty-five (45) feet from a common centre, as established by this Council. And that no property holder shall be permitted to encroach on any street unless all the property holders adjoining, from street to street shall consent to such encroachment in writing; such written consent to be filed with the Clerk of Council. Nor shall any one be permitted to encroach on any street unless all those adjoining, from street to street, shall simultaneously move out in a uniform line, unless by special permission of Council.

Sec. 8. That all property holders who avail themselves of the privilege of this Ordinance be required to put in order and keep up a sidewalk of twelve (12) feet in width, on each side of the street, and plant shade trees between the road bed and sidewalk, and keep the same in proper order. And such property holders shall have removed, at their own expense, the lamp posts now in the streets, to the same relative positions on the new, they now occupy on the old sidewalk; and have the gas pipes so arranged as to communicate with the said lamp posts.

Sec. 9. No building of any description shall ever be erected upon any lot in the city, outside of the original lot line.

Sec. 10. The foregoing Ordinance shall have no reference to any street originally surveyed less than one hundred and twenty feet in width; and shall have no reference to the width of alleys, and no reference to High street; and no street shall be changed in its width so as to interfere with public buildings now erected.

Sec. 11. All property holders availing themselves of the provisions of this Ordinance shall pay into the City Treasury the sum of ten dollars for each lot thus enlarged; and where the lot corners on two streets and the owner encroaches on both streets, such owner shall pay the sum of twenty dollars.

Sec. 12. It shall not be lawful for any person or persons to advance their lots from the original boundary on any of the streets of the City of Macon, without making application to Council, which if granted, shall not be moved out until the amount is paid to the Clerk of Council; and they in every other respect comply with the action of Council on said application.

Sec. 13. All persons who have availed themselves of the Ordinance granting street encroachments, or have received privilege by direct application to Council, and have hitherto neglected or refused to make sidewalks and plant shade trees, or other requirements in compliance with said Ordinance, or direct grant, be forthwith notified by the Marshal to do so; and on failing to comply within thirty (30) days from the notice, then the City Marshal shall cause the same to be done, and return the amount of cost and charges to the Mayor and Aldermen, who shall order the City Treasurer to issue execution for the same against the owner or owners, or agents of the lot or lots, which shall be levied and collected as all executions for taxes on real estate.

Sec. 14. All persons who may hereafter avail themselves of said Encroachment Ordinance, or by direct petition may obtain leave, shall be equally liable to the provisions of this Ordinance.

S

OFFENCES AGAINST MORALITY, PUBLIC SAFETY, AND DECENCY.

SECTION 1. Upon complaint lodged and proof produced to Council of the existence and maintenance of any house of ill fame, or bawdy house, it shall be the duty of the Mayor to give the occupants thereof five days' notice to leave the city, and in case of their failing to do so, by the expiration of that time, he shall require the Marshal and Deputy Marshals forcibly to eject them from the premises, and if necessary, he shall summons a sufficient number of citizens to assist the officers in so doing.

SEC. 2. Any person who shall keep a disorderly house, where noisy, riotous people assemble, to the annoyance of the neighborhood, shall be fined in a sum not exceeding twenty dollars, for each day that the house is so kept.

SEC. 3. All chimneys and stove pipes shall be so constructed as not to endanger the building to which they are attached, or those adjoining, as to fire. And any chimney or stove pipe, which in the opinion of the Council, or a Committee thereof appointed to examine the same, is considered dangerous or a nuisance, shall be removed, or the party shall so alter the same, as to remedy the evil.

SEC. 4. No person shall put in any public pump, pieces of brick, or other substances tending to prevent the free use thereof. No person shall place or cause to be placed near a pump, any barrel, nor wash any clothes, carriages or horses, within twenty feet thereof, under a penalty of five dollars.

SEC. 5. No cellar door shall extend more than six feet into any sidewalk, street or alley, or shall the outer or front part be elevated above the level of such sidewalk, street or alley, nor shall the inner part thereof attached to the dwelling, be elevated more than ten inches above the ground pavement.

SEC. 6. If any person or persons shall cut down or destroy any embankment or other improvement erected by the city authorities for the improvement of the streets or alleys of said city, he or they shall be fined in a sum not exceeding twenty dollars.

SEC. 7. It shall not be lawful for any dray, wagon or carriage to pass through any of the ten foot alleys of the city, unless for the use of persons living on the line of said alleys; and every driver, owner or employer of said drays, wagons or carriages, found driving in, or using the aforesaid alleys, other than for the purposes mentioned, shall be fined in a sum not exceeding five, nor less than two dollars, on conviction before the Mayor.

RAIL ROADS.

It shall not be lawful for any engineer or employee of any Rail Road Company to run any engine or train through any part of the city at a greater rate of speed than five miles per hour, except

ORDINANCES. 59

that portion of the Macon and Western Road from the junction
at the southern portion of the city to the Vineville branch; nor
shall it be lawful to move any cars backwards without having a
guard placed on the backward platform, who shall be furnished
with proper means of giving an alarm in case of danger. Any
person or persons, engineer or fireman, conductor or employee,
guilty of violating this Ordinance, shall be liable to arrest by the
Marshal, Deputy Marshals, or either of the Police officers in special employ of Rail Road Companies, and upon conviction before
the Mayor shall be fined in a sum not less than five, nor more than
fifty dollars, or imprisonment in the city Guard House, or otherwise dealt with, at the discretion of the Mayor.

FAST DRIVING.

It shall not be lawful for any person or persons to ride on
horseback in the city faster than a canter, nor for any coachman
or other person, driving a coach or other carriage, to proceed
faster than a moderate trot, nor for any person driving a loaded
cart, wagon, dray or other carriage used for the transportation
of articles of produce, wares or merchandize, to proceed in a
pace beyond a walk, (except bread carts, which may be driven
in a moderate trot); but all unloaded wagons, carts or drays may
be driven in a moderate trot. *Provided, nevertheless*, the drivers
thereof shall not be allowed to turn corners in any other manner
than walk; and any person violating the provisions of this Ordinance, or owner or owners of such vehicles, shall on conviction be
fined, if a white or free person, in the sum of five dollars; and if
the offender be a slave, his owner or employer shall pay a like
sum, and on refusal to do so, the slave shall be committed to the
Guard House and there kept until his owner or employer shall
have paid said fine together with all expenses; and if a free person
of color, offending against this Ordinance, shall refuse or be unable to pay the aforesaid fine, such free person may be committed to the Guard House, there to remain not exceeding ten days,
or until the aforesaid fine and all expenses shall have been paid.

BARBER SHOPS

No Barber shall keep open his shop on the Sabbath day, on
penalty of a fine at the discretion of the Mayor, not to exceed
twenty dollars.

AGAINST GAMING.

Any person who shall be guilty of violating the laws of this
State relative to gaming houses, gaming tables, or playing and
betting at any game or games played with cards, in the city of
Macon, shall, on proof thereof before the Mayor of the city, be
fined by said Mayor in a sum not exceeding one hundred dollars,

or imprisoned in the common Jail of Bibb county for a space of not more than thirty days, at the discretion of said Mayor.

ORDINANCE AGAINST CARRYING DEADLY WEAPONS.

Be it ordained by the Mayor and Council of the City of Macon, That any white person who shall violate the Statutes of the State of Georgia now in force, relative to carrying about his or her person any deadly weapon mentioned in said Statutes, within the limits of the City of Macon, shall, for each offence, on proof thereof before the Mayor of said city, be fined by said Mayor in a sum of not less than fifty, nor more than one hundred dollars, or imprisoned in the common Jail of Bibb county or the Guard House of said city, for any period not exceeding one month, or both fined and imprisoned as aforesaid, in the discretion of the Mayor. And any slave or free person of color who shall carry about his or her person any deadly weapon of any description— such as are manufactured for purposes of offence or defence— within the limits of said city, shall be punished by whipping and imprisonment in the Guard House of said city, at the discretion of the Mayor—the whipping not to exceed seventy-five lashes, and the imprisonment not to exceed thirty days.

WEIGHTS AND MEASURES.

Section 1. The weights and measures used in the city shall correspond to the standard fixed by law.

Sec. 2. Once in each year the Chief Marshal shall examine and test all weights and measures used for buying and selling in the city, and have all variations therein from the legal standard, promptly corrected; and in case any person required by the Marshal to rectify the weights and measures shall refuse to do the same, or shall be found by said Marshal to have been using false or illegal weights or measures, the name of such person shall be published by order of Council in one of the public gazettes of the city.

Sec. 3. It shall be the duty of the Marshal, under the direction of a Committee to seize all illegal weights and measures in use by any person in the city, and the Marshal shall be entitled to twenty cents for each inspection and stamp, of each set of weights and measures found correct, to be paid by the owner thereof.

TAXES.

Section 1. It shall be the duty, of the Council each year, to pass an ordinance for raising revenue for the current year, impos- ing taxation on all the property of the city, not exceeding the limit authorized by the City Charter.

Sec. 2. All the real estate owned by any person on the first day of January, shall be subject to be assessed by the assessors.

and taxed, and all personal property owned on the first day of January, shall be returned by the person owning the same, or by their agents, under oath, to the Treasurer, and taxed accordingly; *Provided*, That all persons commencing business in the city, after the regular time of returning taxes, shall be liable to be called on for a return of their stock in trade, by the Treasurer, and shall give in and pay the tax thereon rateably, for the portion of the political year that may be unexpired; failing to do which, it shall be the duty of the Treasurer to assess the stock of such person to the best of his ability, and to collect the taxes thereon.

Sec. 3. All persons who shall fail to give in their taxable property other than real estate, within the time specified by the resolution of the Council, shall be double taxed, and t e Treasurer shall issue execution against all persons who shall fail to pay their taxes when required by the Council, to be directed to the Marshal, and bear test in the name of the Mayor.

Sec. 4. All executions issued for taxes shall be collected by the Marshal. All sales under such executions shall be held on the regular Sheriff sales day, and shall be advertised by the Marshal once a week for thirty days, in one of the gazettes of the city. The property sold shall be offered in small parcels, until a bid can be had sufficient to pay the amount, with costs due upon the execution, and the property so offered shall be knocked off to the highest bidder, and the Marshal shall execute to the purchaser titles thereto.

FIRE DEPARTMENT.

Section 1. All Fire Companies that now exist or that may hereafter be created by the City Council shall have power to make and establish a system of By-laws, Rules and Regulations, which they may alter and amend at pleasure, for the management and direction of said Companies; *Provided*, such By-laws, Rules and Regulations, shall not be contrary to the provisions of this, or any other Ordinance of the City of Macon; and such Companies shall have power to fine or expel any of its members for the violation of this Ordinance or the By-laws of said Companies.

Sec. 2. All Fire Companies shall be empowered to take charge and have the care and management of their respective Engine Houses, Engines, Hose, Ladders, Hooks and other apparatus for extinguishing fires, that now belong to, or may hereafter be provided by the City Council, as long as such Companies exist.

Sec. 3. The Fire Companies shall select from their own bodies a Chief Engineer and Assistant Engineer, and shall, after said election, report the same to the City Council, with the names of the individuals so elected, who shall at once enter upon and perform the duties, and possess the powers as shall be hereinafter specified in this Ordinance; *Provided*, said election of Engineers be approved of by the City Council. Elections for said officers to be held annually, on the second Monday in January, except in case of death or resignation, when an election shall be held as soon as practicable thereafter.

Sec. 4. At all fires the Chief Engineer shall have the supreme and absolute command of the Fire Department, and the entire apparatus that may be employed for the extinguishment of fires; and in the absence of the Chief Engineer the above supreme authority shall devolve upon the Assistant Engineer. In case of absence of both the Chief and Assistant Engineer, then the same authority shall devolve upon the senior Foreman present.

Sec. 5. The Chief Engineer shall examine or cause to be examined twice, or oftener if he deems necessary, in each year, into the condition of the Engine Houses, Engines, Hose, and all the apparatus attached to the Fire Department, and make a statement of the same to the City Council or the Committee upon Fire Department, and if any addition or repairs should be required at any time, it shall be his duty in co-operation with said Committee and the Foreman of the Company in whose charge the apparatus to be repaired or added to may be, to have such addition or repair made.

Sec. 6. The Chief Engineer shall order out the Companies of the Fire Department twice a year for inspection and drill.

Sec. 7. The Chief Engineer shall examine, or cause to be examined all Fire Wells and Cisterns belonging to the city as often as he may think necessary; and if the same are not in condition to be used in case of Fire, he shall report the same to the City Council or the Committee on Fire Department.

Sec. 8. The Chief and Assistant Engineer shall, at fires, be distinguished from the rest of the Department by the wearing of a white leather forecap, with the words "Chief," or "Assistant Engineer" upon the front.

FIRE APPARATUS PROTECTED.

Section 1. It shall not be lawful for any person, wilfully and knowingly, to injure or damage in any way or by any means whatever, any engine, hose, hook, ladder or hook and ladder truck or any other implement, material or apparatus of any kind connected with, or used by any Fire Company in this city as a part of their machinery or material for extinguishing or arresting fires. Any white person violating any of the provisions of this section, or who shall procure or induce by any means, whatever, any slave or free person of color to violate any of the provisions thereof, shall on proof thereof before the Mayor of said city, be fined by said Mayor in a sum of money not exceeding one hundred dollars, or imprisoned in the common Jail of Bibb county, or in the Guard House of said city, for any period not exceeding one month, in the discretion of the Mayor. And any slave or free person of color violating the provisions of this section, shall be punished by whipping or imprisonment in the Guard House of said city, or both, at the discretion of the Mayor; the whipping not to exceed one hundred lashes, and the imprisonment not to exceed one month.

SEC. 2. Any white person who shall obstruct with rubbish, or in other way the entrance to any Engine House, used by any of the Fire Companies of said city, or who shall procure any slave or free person of color to do so, may be fined by the Mayor in a sum not exceeding fifty dollars, or imprisoned in the Guard House for not more than ten days. And any slave or free person of color, committing the offence aforesaid, shall be punished by whipping, not to exceed seventy-five lashes in the discretion of the Mayor.

PAY TO FIRE COMPANIES.

The Fire Companies of Macon, Nos. 1, 2, and 3, shall be paid one hundred dollars each per annum, payable quarterly, for the purpose of paying an Engineer employed by them for keeping their Engines and Hose in good order; said Engineers to report to their respective Foremen and the Foremen to the Chief Engineer of the city; no payment to be made to either Company without the endorsement of the Chief Engineer.

FIRE LIMITS.

SECTION 1. That Squares Nos. 18, 19, 20, 21, 22, 23, 38, 39, 40, 41, 42, 43, and 62 in said city, are hereby established and fixed as the Fire Limits.

SEC. 2. It shall not be lawful for any person to build, erect or construct on either of the squares designated in the first section of this Ordinance, any wooden or frame building or other structure of any description, except such as shall be hereinafter specially named, and then only on a strict compliance with the conditions mentioned.

SEC. 3. Any building framed of wood, or having more wood on the outside of the building than that required for door and window frames, doors and stairs, shall be deemed a wooden building, and subject to the penalties of this Ordinance, unless it be one of the buildings or structures hereinafter named and exempted from the operations thereof. And the roof of every piazza and portico (except such as shall be hereinafter exempted from this Ordinance) shall be covered with some material not combustible, otherwise they shall be deemed each to be a wooden building, and subject to the penalties of this Ordinance.

SEC. 4. The following buildings and structures are not inter-dicted by this Ordinance, provided the conditions of their construction and of their being allowed to remain after they are built, are in each instance strictly complied with, to wit:—There may be on each lot embraced within the squres designated in section 1, a wooden well house, provided the same is not more than ten feet in height, and is not used for any other purpose than a well house; and provided no more wood is employed in its construction than may be absolutely necessary to protect a well: There may be on each of said lots a wooden privy, provided the same is not more than ten feet in height, and ten feet in length and width, and is placed at the back part of the lot, as the point most remote from any other building: There may be, also, on each of said lots a wooden shed, not to exceed eight feet in height, nor to exceed eight feet in length or width, provided the same is used for one of the two following purposes, and for those only, to wit—either as a cow shed or as a wash shed; and provided, that in either event no fire shall be used under or within such shed; and there shall never be any chimney or stove put up under or about such shed; and provided further, that such shed shall not be built within fifteen (15) feet of any other building; and there may be on each of said lots, a wooden yard fence for the purpose of enclosing the same; provided said fence does not exceed seven feet in height. If any of the buildings or structures mentioned in this section shall ever be put up in any other manner than that mentioned herein, or after the erection of any building or structure mentioned in this section, any of the conditions of its construction shall be violated or disregarded, such buildings or structures shall thenceforth be subject to the penalties of this Ordinance.

SEC. 5. Should any one erect or cause to be erected on either of the squares designated in section 1, any wooden building or other wooden structure of any kind, except such as are allowed by setion 4 on the conditions therein named, he, she, or they shall be notified by the Marshal to remove the same; and should he, she, or they fail to do so within five days after receiving such notice, the Mayor and Council of said city shall cause the same to be removed at the expense of the owner or owners of such buildings or structures, and which expense shall be collected by execution as in other cases.

SEC. 6. Each and every person who shall violate this Ordinance, or any part of it, shall be fined ten dollars per day for each and every day they fail to regard the notice provided for by section 5.

CITY COMMON, RESERVE, AND PUBLIC PROPERTY.

SECTION 1. Any white person who by himself or a servant, shall haul, or otherwise carry off from the Reserve or Common, any timber or fire-wood, whether such timber or fire-wood be found standing or lying on the ground, shall for such offence, upon conviction, be fined a sum not exceeding twenty dollars. And if any free person of color or slave, acting without the order of his master, shall be guilty of a like offence, he shall be whipped by the Marshal not exceeding thirty-nine lashes; *Provided* that the whipping may be commuted by the Mayor for a pecuniary fine.

Sec. 2. No person shall be permitted to occupy or trespass upon the city common, reserve, any street, alley or any ground or lot owned by the city, under any pretence whatever.

Sec. 3. Any person wishing to obtain a lease upon any part of the city common, shall first publish notice of his intention to apply to the City Council, for one month in each of the city papers, describing the ground applied for, and the use for which it is intended. If no sufficient objection be filed, the Council may, after the expiration of the above specified time, act upon the application, provided that no lease for a longer time than one year, and no sale shall be granted or made without the unanimous vote of the Council who are present.

Sec. 4. The ground in front of the Wesleyan Female College, bounded on the south by Washington street, on the north by two acre lot, No. 10, on the east by Orange street, shall be forever reserved as a public park, and improved only as such, from time to time, as the Mayor and Council of the City of Macon may think proper to have done, or authorize to be done under their direction.

Sec. 5. To establish certain surveys of the city lands made by Augustus Schwaab, Civil Engineer, and to name certain streets in the City of Macon: *Be it ordained by the Mayor and Council of the City of Macon, and it is hereby ordained by the authority of the same,* That the plan of the survey made by Augustus Schwaab, Civil Engineer of that portion of the South-west Common lying below a direct line extending from the lane at the end of Third street to the city boundary, shall hereafter be adopted and established as part of the plan of the City of Macon. And that the division of the Poor House lot (known in the plan of the city as block 16, North-west range) by Schwaab, into sixteen smaller lots, and leaving Madison and Monroe streets, between which they lie, each 130 feet wide, the whole extent of said block from Washington to Forsyth streets, and an alley through the middle of said block, 20 feet wide, the same length; and that the survey of five lots, Nos. 1 to 5 inclusive, lying between Forsyth street and the Macon and Western Railroad, and between the workshops of said Road and Vineville, shall all be adopted and incorporated into the plan of the said City of Macon, and shall hereafter be known and respected accordingly. *And be it further ordained by the authority aforesaid,* That the streets on the Southwest common, as laid out in the survey aforesaid, shall be each

9

100 feet wide, except the one called Division street, which shall be 54 feet wide; and that all the alleys in said survey shall be 20 feet wide, and the streets in said survey shall be known and designated as follows:—The first street beyond the two acre lots running East and West, shall be called Hawthorn street; the next running West and South-east shall be called Tupelo street; the next running parallel shall be called Bay street; the next Hazel street; the next Ash street; the next Elm street; and the next (and outer street) Boundary street, being the present boundary of the city in that direction. And the streets in the said survey running from the two acre lots South-westwardly to the city line, shall be known as follows: The first street leading from the lane at the end of Third street, shall be called Congress street; the next running parallel shall be called McIntosh street, in honor of Gen. Lachlan McIntosh, an early settler of Georgia, and a distinguished officer of the Revolution, also, in honor of the celebrated Indian chief of that name. The next shall be called Elbert street, in honor of Gen. Samuel Elbert, a distinguished officer of the Revolution, and Governor of Georgia. The next shall be called Hammond street, in honor of Col. Sam'l Hammond of the Revolution, a member of Congress from Georgia, and Governor of Missouri. The next shall be called Gilmer street, in honor of George R. Gilmer of this State, who, as member of Congress and Governor, distinguished himself by his able defence of State Rights. The next and last street in said survey shall be called Division street, on account of its dividing the city proper from the reserve. *And be it further ordained,* That the street running from Oglethorpe Encampment westward, in front of the two acre lots, shall be called Oglethorpe street, after the founder of Georgia; and the street next beyond Oak, running from Oglethorpe street up to the hill in front of James A. Ralston's residence, and thence along the brow of the hill to the Columbus road in front of Robert B. Washington's shall, on account of its peculiar shape, be called Arch street. And the road leading out from the upper end of Mulberry street to the city boundary at Vineville, shall be called Georgia Avenue.

SEC. 6. That the plan of the survey made by the Civil Engineer for a new street through Tatnall Square and lots one and four in Block Fifty-six (56) be adopted and established as part of the the plan of the City of Macon:

Be it further ordained, That so much of Johnston street as lies between Ash and Oglethorpe streets be, and the same is hereby closed, and that the new street opened from Ash to Chestnut street, as per plan submitted by the Committee on Public Property to be called "Sparks" street; and that the land taken from Tatnall Square and Johnston street be added to lots three and four in Block Fifty-three and lots three and four, Block Fifty-four.

SEC. 7. Any person who shall in any way molest, injure or damage any property in, or other thing belonging to the city, or who shall cut, carve, injure or damage any of the churches, academics, or other building or other property belonging to the city, or any religious or charitable society or association, or any improvement already made, or that may be hereafter made for the ornament of the streets or other places, by individuals, shall be arrested by the Marshal, and on conviction before the Mayor or any two members of Council, shall be fined not more'than twenty dollars and costs for each and every such offence, or imprisoned in the discretion of the Mayor or any two members of Council.

ROSE HILL CEMETERY.

SECTION 1. A Superintending Committee shall be appointed for Rose Hill and Oak Ridge Cemeteries, (consisting of six persons) by the Mayor and Council, two of whom shall be members of said body. Those from the Council shall be appointed annually; the others shall be a permanent Committee, to be filled by the Council only in case of death, resignation or other causes which a majority thereof may deem sufficient. The permanent committee shall appoint from their number a Superintendent and Treasurer, whose duty it shall be to attend to applications for unsold lots. In their absence or inability to attend to the same, it may be done by the Sexton, under direction from the Superintendent or Treasurer.

SEC. 2. The Superintending Committee may lay out lots at any time when necessary, and assess a price not less than *ten* or more than *thirty* dollars; said lots shall not be larger than 25 by 35, nor less than 20 feet square, except fractional lots, which may be of such dimensions as suit their location. Nor shall they dispose of more than one lot for the use of the same person or family. Titles to all lots shall emanate from the city, and be signed by the Mayor and countersigned by the Clerk of Council and the Treasurer of the Cemeteries.

SEC. 3. The money arising from the sale of lots shall be paid to the Treasurer of the Committee, who shall keep a book of all the receipts and disbursements, and report the same to the Council at their first regular meeting in December or whenever required. He shall disburse the same by order of the Committee for the embellishment and improvement of the grounds, their enclosures, or matters connected therewith, and for no other purpose whatever..

SEC. 4. Persons living out of the city may have the privilege of purchasing lots on the same terms and. conditions as resident citizens.

SEC. 5. Lots may be set apart by the Committee for the use of public institutions of suitable size. Ranges shall also be laid out for the burial of strangers and others who may not purchase lots.

Sec. 6. No lot shall be cleared of its growth other than the undergrowth by the owner, except under the superintendence or direction of one or more of the Superintending Committee—all rubbish that may be created by the clearing up or improvement of a lot, shall be burnt or removed by the owner within forty-eight hours. No fire shall be kindled where it may injure the standing growth in or about any of the lots or other parts of the grounds, under a penalty for such offence of not less than five or more than twenty dollars, on conviction before the Mayor.

Sec. 7. The Treasurer and Sexton shall keep a plan of the grounds for public inspection, which shall be furnished them with all the lots and ranges properly numbered, with the names of the owners. The Sexton shall see that the numbers are kept up on the lots or stakes, or in some other suitable manner, which numbers shall be furnished him by the Superintending Committee. He shall keep a book of all interments, in which shall be stated the name, age, nativity, and cause of death as near as practicable, with the number of the lot—or if buried in the strangers range—with the number of the grave. And it shall further be his duty to report to Council a monthly transcript of such record, or in default shall be subject, on conviction to a penalty of five dollars.

Sec. 8. Any lot that may be sold if the terms are not complied with shall, if not occupied, revert again to the control of the Superintending Committee, or if occupied in part, the remaining portion may be again disposed of, and should the owner of any unoccupied lot remove from the city, without transfering his rights to another, the said lots shall revert in like manner at the end of three years.

Sec. 9. The Sexton shall inter all bodies in a grave of not less than five feet in depth, or in a vault, but in no case shall he permit a body to remain above ground enclosed with brick or other materials. He shall not suffer any piles of earth, brick, mortar beds or rubbish of any kind to remain on the ground longer than twenty-four hours after an interment or the completion of any work incident to a burial; for such neglect he shall be subject to to a fine, on conviction before the Mayor, of not less than five nor more than ten dollars, at the discretion of the Mayor.

Sec. 10. It shall be the duty of the Clerk of Council to copy the monthly report of the Sexton in a well bound book kept for that purpose in his office.

Sec. 11. It shall not be lawful for any person to inter a body in either Rose Hill or Oak Ridge Cemeteries, or remove a body which has been or shall hereafter be interred in either of said Cemeteries, from its place of interment, without the knowledge or presence of the Sexton. Any white person offending against any of the provisions of this section, or who shall in any way procure or induce any slave or free person of color to offend against the same, shall be fined by the Mayor of said city in a sum not less than fifty, nor more than one hundred dollars, or imprisoned in the common Jail of Bibb county, or the Guard House of said city for the space of one month, or shall be both fined and imprisoned as aforesaid at the discretion of the Mayor. And any slave or free person of color violating any of the provisions of this section, shall be punished by whipping or confinement in the Guard House, of said city, or both, in the discretion of the Mayor.

GRANTING RESERVE TO CEMETERY.

SECTION 1. That portion of the City Common bounded as follows, shall be set aside and perpetually reserved free and exempt from sale or lease forever, to wit:

Commencing at the upper end of Wharf street, adjoining Dr. Pye's lot, known as lot number seventeen, between Orange and College streets, thence running down Wharf street to the intersection of Franklin street, then along Franklin street to the intersection of Rose street, thence down Rose street to a branch, thence along the line and run of said branch to the Ocmulgee river, on the line of low water mark of said river, until it strikes the line of Rose Hill Cemetery, thence along the line of Rose Hill Cemetery, until it reaches Orange street, thence to the starting point at the upper end of Wharf street, be the same more or less.

SEC. 2. The front line of said Cemetery, as now laid off and fenced, shall be made perpetual as the boundaries thereof; and that no interments be allowed in said reserve.

PROTECTION, ETC., TO ROSE HILL AND OAK RIDGE CEMETERIES.

SECTION 1. If any persons shall fire a gun, pistol, or any other fire arms within the enclosure of either of said Cemeteries, unless it be at a funeral in honor of the dead, they shall be subject to a fine not exceeding twenty dollars.

SEC. 2. If any person shall mutilate or in any manner deface a monument, fence or other enclosures in said Cemeteries, they shall be subject to a fine of twenty dollars; and if any person shall dig up, remove or destroy any shrubbery or trees within the enclosure of Rose Hill or Oak Ridge Cemeteries, or upon the reserved land around said Cemeteries, unless by permission of the Superintendent, or some one of the permanent Committee, they shall be subject to a fine of not more than ten, or less than five dollars, at the discretion of the Mayor.

SEC. 3. For the better protection of the flowers, shrubbery and plants in Rose Hill Cemetery, it shall not be lawful for any person or persons to break down or gather any wild or cultivated flowers in said Cemetery, under a penalty of five dollars, one half to go to the informers; and it shall be the duty of the Sexton to inform persons visiting the grounds, of the existence of this Ordinance. and report all violations of the same that come to his knowledge.

FISH, PUBLIC GROUNDS, ETC.

Section 1. Any person who shall be guilty of taking, catching, molesting or injuring the fish in any lake or pond of water in any of the Cemeteries under the control of the City Council of. Macon, or of molesting or injuring, in any improper manner, the public grounds, improvements, natural or other growth belonging or appertaining thereto, shall, on conviction, be fined by the Mayor in a sum not more than fifty dollars or imprisoned in the common Jail of Bibb county, or in the Guard House of the city, not exceeding one month, at the discretion of the Mayor. And any slave or free person of color, who shall violate any portion of this Ordinance, shall, upon conviction, receive not exceeding seventy-five lashes.

Sec. 2. And be it further ordained, that the penalties provided for the foregoing offences shall attach to any and all violations of the Ordinances heretofore passed for the protection of said Cemeteries, except as to violations of the Ordinance relative to interring and disinterring bodies; and that all said Ordinances shall hereafter extend to all said Cemeteries.

TRIAL OF OFFENDERS.

Section 1. Every person who is charged with any offence shall be summoned in writing to appear before the Mayor or City Council, as the case may be, and answer the charges alleged against him or her; which summons shall be served in person by the Marshal or Polic, and shall specify the time and place of trial.

In case of the failure or refusal of any party to appear, it shall be the duty of the Police to arrest him or her, and to bring them to trial.

Sec. 2. All subpœnas for witnesses shall be issued and signed by the Clerk of Council; and any person who shall fail to appear as a witness, when summoned, shall, unless a satisfactory excuse be given, be fined in the sum of twenty dollars.

Sec. 3. When a fine shall have been imposed by the Mayor, or by the Mayor and Council, the offender shall remain in custody until the fine is paid; or the Mayor may, in his discretion, order the Clerk to issue an execution for the fine, which shall be directed to and collected by the Marshal, by levy and sale of the lands, tenements, goods and chattels of the offender.

Sec. 4. All sales, under such executions, shall be had on the regular Sheriff sales day, and personal goods shall be advertised fifteen days, and real estate thirty days before the day of sale.

SEC. 5. In all cases in which the penalty for violating any ordinance of the city is not specified, the offender, if a white person, shall be fined at the discretion of the Mayor, not exceeding twenty dollars; and if a negro, he or she shall be punished as the Mayor may direct.

AN ORDINANCE

To adopt the Compilation of the Acts of Incorporation and Ordinances of the City of Macon, made by Mr. RICHARD CURD, and to repeal Ordinances conflicting therewith or not contained in the same.

SECTION 1. *Be it ordained by the Mayor and Council of the City of Macon, and it is hereby ordained by the authority of the same,* That all the Ordinances and By-laws contained in said compilation be and they are hereby ratified and confirmed and declared to be in full force and effect.

SEC. 2. *Be it further ordained,* That said Compilation be published under the supervision of the Finance Committee with as little delay as practicable.

APPENDIX.

MANUFACTURES.

An Ordinance to encourage Manufacturing and the Mechanic Arts. May 18, 1849.

SECTION 1. *Be it ordained by the Mayor and City Council of the City of Macon,* That the lots and buildings hereafter erected thereon, and the stock in trade hereafter used or employed immediately in and about the business of manufacturing, by any individual or company, of cotton, wool, paper, leather and flour, within the corporate limits of the City of Macon, shall be exempt from taxation for and during the term of ten years from the passage of this Ordinance; *Provided,* That nothing herein contained shall exempt from taxation any goods, wares or merchandize, which may be kept for barter or sale by any person or company as above, excepting only fabrics and articles of their own manufacture.

SEC. 2. *And be it further ordained,* That nothing shall be considered stock in trade, as the words are used in the first section of this Ordinance, but capital stock, or money used by any individual or company immediately in the business of manufacturing, and the necessary machinery and fabrics manufactured.

SEC. 3. *And be it further ordained,* That no tannery or other branch of manufacturing, calculated to prove a nuisance, or interfere with the health or comfort of the citizens, shall be established within the business district of the city, or in any place by which the neighbors will be annoyed, or their health and comfort interfered with.

BUILDING AND LOAN ASSOCIATION.

Be it ordained, &c., That from and after the passage of this Ordinance, the Macon Building and Loan Association be, and they are hereby released and exempted from the payment of taxes to the city on any money they now or may hereafter have loaned at interest during their existence as a Building and Loan Association.

Passed March 24, 1854.

BONDS TO PAY CITY DEBT.

Be it ordained, &c., That the Mayor be authorized to issue the Bonds of the City of Macon to the amount of forty thousand dollars, payable annually, on the 1st day of November, 1856, '57, '58, '59, '60, '61, '62 and '63, pledging as security for the payment of said Bonds, the annuity of five thousand dollars coming to the city under contract on the 1st day of October, of every year, for crossing the Ocmulgee river, from the Central, South-western, and Macon and Western Railroad Companies,—said Bonds to be in sums as follows: those payable on the 1st day of November, 1856, in sums of One Thousand Dollars each, and those payable on the 1st day of November, 1857, '58, '59, '60, '61, '62 and '63, in sums of Five Hundred Dollars each, bearing an interest of 7 per cent., payable semi-annually, on the 1st day of May and the 1st day of November of each year, whenever negotiated according to the coupons or interest warrants to be annexed to the Bonds.

SEC. 2. *And be it further ordained*, That for and in consideration of the endorsement of the principal of said Bonds by the Central, South-western, and Macon and Western Railroad Companies, the annuity coming to the city from said Companies of Five Thousand Dollars, for the years 1857, '58, '59, '60, '61, '62 and '63, under a contract for crossing the Ocmulgee river, be and the same is hereby transferred to the President of the Central Railroad and Banking Company, with full authority to receive, receipt for, and apply to the payment of the said Bonds at maturity.

SEC. 3. *And be it further ordained*, That the proceeds of or the moneys arising from the sale of said Bonds, shall be applied exclusively to the payment of the City Bonds, due and payable in the city of New York, on the 15th day of November next.

SEC. 4. *And be it further ordained*, That the Mayor be and is hereby authorized to make sale of said Bonds in such sums and in such manner as he may deem best for the interest of the city.

Passed June 19, 1855.

CITY BONDS FOR CITY HALL.

SECTION 1. *Be it ordained, &c.*, That the Mayor be authorized to issue the bonds of the city to the amount of Thirty Thousand dollars, payable annually, on the 1st day of November, 1864, '65, '66, '67, '68, and '69, pledging as security for the payment of said Bonds, the annuity coming to the city, under contract, on the 1st day of October every year, for crossing the Ocmulgee river, from the Central, South western and Macon and Western Railroad Companies—said Bonds to be in sums as follows: those payable on the 1st day of November, 1864, '65, in sums of One hundred dollars each, and those payable on the 1st day of November, 1866, '67, '68, and 1869, in sums of Five hundred dollars, each, bearing an interest of 7 per cent. payable, semi-annually on the 1st day of May, and on the 1st day of November, of each year, wherever negotiated according to the coupons or interest warrants to be annexed to the Bonds.

Sec. 2. *And be it further ordained*, That the proceeds of the moneys arising from the sale of said Bonds shall be applied exclusively to the payment of the cost of building a new City Hall, and used for no other purpose whatever.

Sec. 3. *And be it further ordained*, That the Mayor be and he is hereby authorized to make sale of said Bonds in such sums and in such manner as he may deem best for the interest of the city.

Passed February 5, 1856.

RAIL ROAD STOCK.

An Ordinance to authorize a Subscription for Stock in a Rail Road from War-renton to Macon, and to provide for the payment of the same.

Whereas, At a public meeting of the citizens of Macon, had and held at the Council Chamber in said City, on December 6, 1853, the Mayor and Council of the City of Macon were by said meeting unanimously instructed to subscribe $100,000 to the Stock of the contemplated Rail Road from Warrenton to Macon, and issue therefor Bonds of the city, to be due in ten or fifteen years after date, as the Council may deem best, the Bonds bearing seven per cent. interest, payable on the first of December in each year—upon condition that the said Bonds shall be received at par by said Company with an hypothecation of the Stock for their redemption, and upon the further condition that the proposed Rail Road be built from Warrenton to Macon:

Section 1. *Be it therefore ordained, &c.*, That the Mayor of said city is hereby authorized and requested to subscribe in behalf of the city for one hundred thousand dollars of the Stock of said Rail Road from Warrenton to Macon upon the terms herein set forth and prescribed.

Sec. 2. *And be it further ordained by the authority aforesaid,* That his Honor, the Mayor of said city, be, and he is hereby authorized to make and issue in the name and in behalf of the City of Macon, Bonds of convenient amounts, not exceeding in the aggregate the sum of one hundred thousand dollars, required by him in his official capacity, countersigned by the Clerk of Council, and sealed with the corporate seal of said city, payable $50,000 in ten, and $50,000 in fifteen years after date, with interest at the rate of seven per cent. per annum, payable yearly on the first day of December in each year; the interest on said Bonds to begin on the dates on which the installments of said stock may be required to be paid by the Commissioners or Directors of said Rail Road Company.

Sec. 3. *And be it further ordained*, That a sufficient amount of said Bonds be, from time to time, delivered to said Rail Road Company in payment of the instalments of said Stock as the same may be called in and fall due, the City of Macon receiving the proper scrip for all such payments.

Passed Dec. 9, 1853.

CITY BONDS FOR STOCK IN MACON AND BRUNSWICK RAIL ROAD.

Section 1. *Be it ordained, &c.*, That the Mayor be authorized to issue the Bonds of the City of Macon to the amount of Two hundred thousand dollars—of Five hundred dollars each: Five thousand dollars to be made payable on the first day of November in each of the years 1860, '61, '62, '63, '64 and '66; and Ten thousand dollars on the first day of November in each of the years 1865, '67, '68, '69, '70, '71, '72, '74, '75, '76, '78, '79, '80, '81, '82 and '83; said Bonds to bear interest at the rate of seven per cent. per annum after the first day of July, 1860, and said interest payable semi-annually, on the first day of May and November in each year, for which coupons, or interest warrants are to be attached to the Bonds.

Sec. 2. *Be it further ordained*, That the Mayor sign, and the Clerk countersign said Bonds, and the Clerk of Council sign the coupons, or interest warrants attached thereto, and that when they are properly executed, that the Mayor deliver them to the Macon and Brunswick Rail Road Company in payment for the Stock subscribed for, by the City of Macon, in said Rail Road Company.

Passed Sept. 13, 1859.

NEW CITY SEAL.

An Ordinance to change Corporate Seal of the City of Macon.

Section 1. *Be it ordained by the City Council of the City of Macon, and it is hereby ordained by the authority of the same*, That from and after the passage of this Ordinance the Corporate Seal of the City of Macon shall be as follows:

A round Seal with a device containing a full bolled cotton plant in bold relief and a train of Rail Road cars in the rear, surrounded by the inscription: "*Ædes, Mores Legesque Custodiat*," and under the device, the words "*Corpus Politicum*."

Sec. 2. That all Ordinances or parts of Ordinances militating against this Ordinance, be, and the same are hereby repealed.

Passed July 10, 1856.

RESOLUTIONS.

Resolved, That the Report of the Committee appointed to fix upon the details in regard to the connection of the different Rail Roads within the limits of this city, at a common Depot, be approved and adopted as the action of the Mayor and Council of this city, and that his honor the Mayor be requested to have a contract drawn up embracing the terms and conditions set forth in the said Report, and submit the same to the several Rail Road Companies, for their ratification and signature in due and legal form.

Resolved, That the Mayor be requested to incorporate in the contract with the Rail Road Companies a clause prohibiting said Company from charging toll on the bridge which they may construct across the river, or using said bridge for any other than ordinary Rail Road purposes.

CONTRACT WITH THE RAIL ROAD COMPANIES.

STATE OF GEORGIA, *Bibb County.*

WHEREAS, In and by an Act of the General Assembly of the State of Georgia, approved the 11th day of February, eighteen hundred and fifty, (1850,) it was provided that it should be lawful for the "Central Railroad and Banking Company of Georgia," the "Macon and Western Railroad Company," and the "Southwestern Railroad Company," to unite their respective Railroads in one common depot, at, near or within the City of Macon, "so that the cars of the respective roads might pass from one road to another uninterruptedly," upon either of the several conditions in said Act specified; one of which was, "the consent of the Corporation of the said City of Macon, for said roads to be united within said corporate limits:" And whereas, The Mayor and Council of the City of Macon have come to an understanding and agreement with said Companies as to the mode and manner of said junction, and as to the terms and conditions of their consent to the said union of the Railroads of said three Companies within the city of Macon:

Now, this Indenture, made this the 24th day of January, eighteen hundred and fifty-one, by and between the Mayor and Council of the City of Macon, for itself and on the behalf of all persons who are or shall become, interested in the provisions hereof, of the one part, and the Central Railroad and Banking Company of Georgia, the Macon and Western Railroad Company, and the South-western Railroad Company of the other part: WITNESSETH, That the Mayor and Council of the City of Macon, for and in consideration of the covenants hereinafter contained, to be observed, kept and performed by the said Companies, and each of them, have granted, bargained, sold, aliened and conveyed, and doth by these presents grant, bargain, sell, alien and convey unto said Companies, the right, power and privilege of making said connection, by running the tracks of their respective Railroads as follows:—Branching from the Central Railroad and Banking Company's Railroad, a short distance below their depot in East Macon, curving into and crossing the river (Ocmulgee) opposite the North-east end of the street, known in the plan of said city as Sixth street, and running up Sixth street to the South-western Railroad Company's present Depot, on square seventy-nine, (79,) in the City of Macon—making at present a Passenger Depot at the intersection of Mulberry and Sixth streets, (near the Court-house square,) while the Macon and Western Railroad Company's Railroad is to unite in said connection, by branching from its Railroad a short distance above their present work-shops, and running through the City Common and crossing the Columbus road in the rear of the residences of John D. Gray and Robert B. Washington, and down along the bottom land of the branch (known as Roger's branch) near Troup Hill, and then curving into the Railroad of the South-western Railroad Company, with the understanding that if the route, as to the bottom lands of said branch, should prove objectionable, then the nearest practicable line within the City Common is to be substituted. And with the further understanding that the permanent common depot (hereby allowed) when established, shall be located either on the line of route herein pointed out, or within such convenient distance from said line of route and within the limits of the City of Macon, as may hereafter be agreed upon by and between the parties to this contract.

And the Mayor and Council of the City of Macon also by these presents, grants, bargains, sells and conveys unto the said three Companies, the right and privilege of using and occupying so much of the said Sixth and Mulberry streets at their intersection, as may be necessary for erecting, maintaining and keeping a common depot of said Companies, so that the tracks of their several Railroads shall unite and run into each other—reserving and leaving out the needful space along the course of each of said streets and around the depot, for the free passage of carriages, drays, and other vehicles; *Provided*, That the space so to be reserved for vehicles may be substituted for the like needful space around the Depot, if ever enlarged by the purchase and addition thereto of lands adjacent to said Depot—

To have and to hold unto said three Companies and their successors, so much of the said streets and City Common and City lots of the said city, as are hereinbefore described, as a part of their works respectively, (as they may among themselves adjust and arrange,) without any manner of molestation or hindrance whatever by the Mayor and Council of the City of Macon, during the faithful observance of this contract by said three Companies, and each of them.

And the said three Companies on their part, in consideration of the aforesaid premises, hereby jointly and severally, agree, promise and covenant as follows: That they will annually, at the expiration of each twelve months, pay to the said Mayor and Council of the City of Macon, the sum of five thousand dollars, so long as the said privilege of crossing the river at the place and in the manner aforesaid, and connecting at a common depot as aforesaid, shall be used and enjoyed by said Companies or any two of them—the said time to be computed and begin to run from the day that any two of said Companies may each have run a car to said common depot—and if said Companies or any one of them shall at an earlier day commence their business of carrying freight or passengers across the river, then to date and run from such earlier day. And said three Companies further covenant and agree with the Mayor and Council of the City of Macon, for itself and on the behalf of all persons who, as aforesaid, (as shippers of produce or otherwise,) may be, or become interested in the faithful observance of this particular covenant, that from and immediately after the " crossing and connection " herein contemplated shall take place, the rates of freight between Griffin and Savannah, [meaning the city of Griffin on the Macon and Western Railroad Company's Railroad, and the town of Oglethorpe on the line of the road of the South-western Railroad Company] shall be and remain always, at least one-fifth more in the respective cases, than the rates of freight between Macon and Savannah—so that no improper discrimination shall be made against Macon by said Railroad Companies, in favor of either of said towns or cities. And it is further covenanted and agreed by said three Companies, that they will, as to the extension of their respective Railroads herein contemplated, make, and during the use of said extension, maintain, suitable crossings of all streets, alleys, lawfully established roads, (and of such streets alleys and roads as the Mayor and Council of the City of Macon may hereafter establish,) over and across which their, or either of their extended tracks may pass in forming said junction, so as not to make any such road, street or alley, in any manner worse by reason of said several extensions, or of either of them.

And it is further covenanted and agreed by said three Companies, that no toll shall be charged for crossing the bridge (over the Ocmulgee) to be built under this contract, and that no free crossing thereat shall be allowed other than such as may for the time being be allowed at the bridge of the City of Macon, and that said Railroad bridge shall not be used for any other than ordinary legitimate Railroad purposes.

And it is hereby understood and mutually agreed by the parties hereto, that nothing in the nature of this contract is to interfere with the lawful taxing power of the Mayor and Council of the City of Macon over the depot buildings, and other property of said Companies, and of each of them, the right of taxing said property being hereby reserved

In testimony whereof, The Mayor of said city and the President of the aforesaid three Companies, have affixed their signatures to this agreement in quadruplicate, with their respective corporate seals duly attested.

J. H. R. WASHINGTON,
Mayor of the City of Macon.

R. R. CUYLER,
President C. R. R. and Banking Co.

ISAAC SCOTT,
President Macon and Western R. R. Co.

L. O. REYNOLDS,
President South western R. R. Co.

[L. S.] Attest, A. R. FREEMAN, c. c.

[L. S.] Attest, SOLOMON COHEN, Cashier.

R. W. ADAMS,

W. R. BULLOCH, N. P.

[L. S.] Attest, IRA H. TAYLOR, Sec.

[L. S.] Attest, W. S. HOLT, Sec.

CONTRACT WITH THE CONFEDERATE STATES.

STATE OF GEORGIA, *Bibb County.*

THIS INDENTURE, made the third day of October, in the year of our Lord one thousand eight hundred and sixty-two, between the Mayor and Council of the City of Macon, State and county aforesaid, of the first part, and the Confederate States of America, of the second part, witnesseth:

That the said Mayor and Council, in testimony of the patriotic devotion of the people of Macon to the Government of their choice, and the cause of the country in her struggle for life, liberty and independence, as well as with a view to the benefit likely to arise from the establishment of an Armory in our midst, and in further consideration of the sum of five dollars in hand paid, at and before the sealing and delivery of these presents, the receipt whereof is hereby acknowledged: have granted, bargained and sold, and by these presents do grant, bargain, sell and convey to the Confederate States of America, for the purpose of erecting on the same an Armory of the said States for the manufacture of small arms necessary for their use, and for no other purposes, except such as are usually and properly connected with the same, unless the consent of the then existing Mayor and Council shall have first been had and obtained; all that lot or parcel of land, lying and being situated within the corporate limits of said city, and bounded on three sides by Calhoun, Hazel and Lamar streets, and on the other by the line of the Macon and Western Railroad, along which it is conditioned that a street of at least one hundred and twenty-five feet width shall be made and maintained in good condition, free for public use, and to secure easy access to the city from parts and places beyond said Armory or the line of the said Railroad, the whole containing an area of about forty-three acres, be the same more or less:

To Have and to Hold, the said lot or parcel of land, with all and singular the rights, members and appurtenances thereto appertaining or belonging, for the uses specified as aforesaid, to the Confederate States of America, so long as it shall be deemed the interest of said States to devote it to said uses, and not longer; and the said Mayor and Council, the said specified premises, conditioned as aforesaid, to the Confederate States of America, against the said Mayor and Council, their successors or assigns, and against all and every other person or persons, shall and will warrant and forever defend, by virtue of these presents.

In Testimony whereof, The said party of the first part hath by resolution caused these presents to be subscribed by the Mayor of the City of Macon, and the Common Seal of said city to be hereunto affixed by the Clerk of said city, and these presents to be delivered, the day and year first above written.

     (Signed)   M. S. THOMSON, *Mayor.*

Rich'd Curd, C. C.

RULES OF COUNCIL.

1. Meetings of the Council shall be held regularly every Friday, at 7 oclock, P. M., unless otherwise ordered by the Council. Special meetings may be called by the Mayor, of which the Marshal shall give the members of Council notice.

2. The Mayor and four members of Council shall constitute a quorum for the transaction of business.

3. When any ordinance, or motion for the alteration of an ordinance shall be submitted to the Council, it shall be read at the meeting when the same is proposed, but shall not be acted upon at that time without the unanimous consent of the Council. At the subsequent meeting the ordinance or amendment proposed shall be again read, and be subject to such revision or alteration, as the Council may deem proper. The vote, unless otherwise ordered, shall be taken on each section separately; and after the several sections shall have been acted on, then the vote shall be taken upon the entire ordinance.

4. At the commencement of each regular meeting, the Clerk shall read the proceedings of the last meeting; and if the minutes are correct, they will be signed by the Mayor. And at the close of each meeting the Mayor shall adjourn the Council to the time agreed on.

5. The following order shall be observed in the transaction of business:

    1. Reading of the Minutes.
    2. Information Docket.
    3. Reports from Standing Committees—Finance first.
    4. Reports from Select Committees.
    5. Reports from Officers.
    6. Resolutions, Orders and Ordinances.
    7. Accounts and Salaries.
    8. Business of last Meeting lying over.

6. Whenever it shall be required by one or more members, the yeas and nays shall be recorded.

7. All questions shall be put by the Mayor, or in his absence by the *Mayor pro tem.*; those in favor of the question by saying aye; those against it, no. Members voting *viva voce*; majorities determining all questions. The Mayor may, at discretion, call any member to take the chair, to allow him to address the Council, or make a motion.

8. All elections to be by ballot.

9. All Reports and Resolutions, unless for adjournment, shall be submitted in writing.

10. Each member, when the Board is convened and organized for business, when speaking, shall rise and address the Chairman.

11. The duties of the Clerk shall in no instance be performed by proxy or substitute, except in case of sickness, or by consent of the Mayor and Council by resolution.

12. It shall be the duty of the Clerk of Council and Marshal to attend all meetings of this Board; and in case of absence they shall be fined in the sum of five dollars, unless a reasonable excuse be given.

13. For non-attendance, or other neglect of duty of all officers of Council, they will be fined in such sum as the Mayor and Council, or a majority of them may determine.

14. No interruptions will be permitted while a member is speaking on such matters as may be before Council, unless for explanation

15. Applications, petitions, or other communications to Council must be made in writing, and in all cases the same must be referred to a committee previous to action.

16. These rules shall be considered binding on the Council, and liable to alteration or addition only by motion, submitted at a meeting previous to a vote on the question.

17. Before the minutes of any preceding meeting of Council are confirmed, any member may move to reconsider any question, motion, resolution, or other matter or thing in the minutes of such previous meeting contained, and if such reconsideration be voted for by a majority of the members present, the subject-matter of such reconsideration shall be the first business in order to be disposed of.

INDEX TO CHARTER.

INDEX TO ORDINANCES.

   12

ERRATA.—An omission exists in the Ordinance under the head of "Police," page 27, section 1. It should read

SECTION 1. *Be it ordained, &c.,* That the police force of the city shall consist of a Marshal and one or more Deputy Marshals, and six *or more* Police-men. The Mayor shall appoint two of the Police-men to act as lieutenants.

www.ingramcontent.com/pod-product-compliance
Lightning Source LLC
Chambersburg PA
CBHW032356280326
41935CB00008B/599

* 9 7 8 3 3 3 7 3 0 1 9 4 1 *